D1152979

Geoff Tibballs is the author of a number of bestselling humour and sports books, including *The Mammoth Book of Jokes, Great Sporting Failures, Great Sporting Eccentrics* and *The Bowler's Holding, the Batsman's Willey*. Among his recent titles are *The Mammoth Book of Weird Records* and *The World's 100 Weirdest Museums*. Before becoming an armchair sportsman, he used to give a passable imitation of a frustrated golfer and a static tennis player. He has absolutely no ambition to chase a large cheese down a steep hill.

Other titles

The World's 100 Weirdest Sporting Events

From Gravy Wrestling in Lancashire to Wife Carrying in Finland

GEOFF TIBBALLS

ROBINSON

ROBINSON

First published in Great Britain in 2017 by Robinson

A CIP catalogue record for this book is available from the British Library

ISBN: 978-1-47214-049-4

Typeset in Nexus Serif by Hewer Text UK Ltd, Edinburgh
Printed and bound in Great Britain by Clays Ltd, St Ives plc

Papers used by Robinson are from well-managed
forests and other responsible sources

MIX
Paper from
responsible sources
FSC® C104740

Robinson
An imprint of
Little, Brown Book Group
Carmelite House
50 Victoria Embankment
London EC4Y 0DZ

An Hachette UK Company
www.hachette.co.uk

www.littlebrown.co.uk

CONTENTS

CHAPTER TWO: QUIRKY GAMES

CHAPTER THREE: TRIVIAL PURSUITS

CHAPTER FOUR: TAKING IT TO EXTREMES

CHAPTER FIVE: TARGET PRACTICE

CHAPTER SIX: FEATS OF STRENGTH

CHAPTER SEVEN: BOGGED DOWN

CHAPTER EIGHT: CHILLING OUT

CHAPTER NINE: ALL CREATURES GREAT AND SMALL

INTRODUCTION

When we think of the world's great sporting events, we tend to focus on spectacles such as the World Cup, the Olympics, the Derby, the Monaco Grand Prix or the University Boat Race. Yet there is also an alternative world of competition where participants risk life, limb and often dignity for meagre rewards in truly weird sporting pursuits. Step forward the Indonesian sport of sepak bola api, a variation of football in which the barefoot players kick a ball that is on fire; Germany's Mud Olympics, at which competitors play soccer, volleyball and handball while knee-deep in mud; Oregon's Pig-N-Ford Races where drivers speed around the track while carrying a live pig under one arm; and Australia's variation of the Boat Race, the Henley-on-Todd River Race, where, instead of rowing, teams carry their boats along the dry bed of the River Todd.

Eccentricity truly comes into its own on the field of sport, and here I have selected 100 of the world's weirdest sports events. They include the grotesque (the national sport of Afghanistan is buzkashi, in which riders on horseback aim to drag the headless carcass of a dead goat towards their opponents' goal), the dangerous (instead of using their bare hands, Japanese deathmatch wrestlers batter each other with glass light tubes, fire extinguishers or baseball bats covered in barbed wire), and the downright daft in the form of the World Black Pudding Throwing Championships, the World Flounder Tramping Championships, the World Gravy Wrestling Championships, the Shin Kicking World Championships and the Wife Carrying World Championships. If there is a world championship for wife swapping, it is almost certainly held behind closed doors.

Races are staged in all kinds of transportation. Canada is home to the Great Klondike International Outhouse Race (for portable toilets), the World Championship Bathtub Race, and pumpkin kayaking; Colorado hosts the annual Emma Crawford Coffin Races; Germany has the World Wok Racing Championships (for those who have always wanted to know what it would feel like to speed down a bobsled run in a frying pan), and the pride of Yorkshire is the Great Knaresborough Bed Race, where teams push a bed (containing a human occupant) along a 2.4-mile course that requires a wet crossing of the River Nidd.

Animals feature heavily, too. As well as traditional races for ostriches (complete with jockeys), cockroaches (no jockey required), snails, and Australia's splendid Dachshund Dash, rubber-duck racing is one of the fastest growing sports of recent years, with events being held in several countries. Other competitions test an animal's ability to do more than just run or float, such as dog surfing, camel wrestling, rabbit show jumping and pig diving. It is not beyond the realms of possibility that at some time in the future we may be treated to synchronised pig diving.

Although the plunging porkers might disagree, the appeal of many of these sports is enhanced by taking part. If cheese rolling or volcano boarding are too energetic for your taste, ice golf or underwater ice hockey too uncomfortable, and lingerie football wouldn't show off your legs to best effect, you could always enjoy more leisurely pursuits like Rock Paper Scissors, pooh sticks or worm charming. If, on the other hand, you prefer a watching brief, you could try your hand at cow-pat bingo, an international contest where a field is divided into numbered squares, and contestants bet on which square the cow will take a poop. It is probably the only occasion in life when you can make money from one number two on top of another.

CHAPTER ONE
WACKY RACES

BEER MILE WORLD CHAMPIONSHIP, AUSTIN, TEXAS, USA

To many people, 'fun run' is one of the world's great oxymorons along with 'head butt', 'crash landing' and 'military intelligence'. But how much more enjoyable and therefore mentally beneficial would a run be if it were broken up by the occasional beer, say every lap? That is the premise of the beer mile, a running race that takes place around a standard athletics track but which is started not by a gun, but by the swift consumption of a can or bottle of beer. Further beers are downed in a designated zone at the end of laps one, two and three, the eventual winner being the first competitor to finish four laps and four beers. Whereas track races other than short sprints traditionally have staggered starts, the beer mile is unique in often having a staggered finish.

The beer mile originated on the college campuses of North America in the late 1980s. As its popularity spread among thirsty students, an official set of rules, 'The Kingston Rules' (named after a city in Ontario), was drawn up. These rules stipulated that the beer drunk must be no less than twelve ounces in size and must be a minimum of five per cent alcohol. Cans must be drunk from the tab on the top and must not have been tampered with in any way. This is to prevent unscrupulous athletes deliberately puncturing the can beforehand so that there is less to drink.

Lastly, any competitor who vomits before the finish must run an extra lap. These regulations have generally been adopted across the world, although in Britain runners sometimes down a whole pint before each lap and therefore find it necessary to waive the no-vomiting rule. Apparently, the secret of success is to burp out as much beer as possible in the first few strides of each lap, allowing the run to continue unhindered by excess gas.

In the same way that the four-minute barrier proved elusive for decades to dry milers, so beer milers struggled to break five minutes – that is until 27 April 2014 when Californian athlete James 'the Beast' Nielsen recorded a time of 4:57.1. It was almost sixty years to the day since Roger Bannister had run the first non-alcoholic four-minute mile, although for some reason the Englishman's feat still occupies a more prominent place in athletics history. Nielsen's breakthrough was followed at the end of that year by the inaugural staging of the Beer Mile World Championship in Austin, Texas. The men's race was won by Canadian Corey Gallagher in 5:00.23 and the women's event by American Beth Herndon in 6:17.8. This has since become an annual competition and is now one of the key dates in the calendar for beer milers.

Meanwhile, in August 2015, Nielsen helped organise the first Beer Mile World Classic in San Francisco. It was won by Canadian Lewis Kent, who had finished a disappointing fifth in Austin. He blamed the beer, telling ESPN: 'I went with Budweiser Platinum, but I should have brought my own. This time, I travelled with Amsterdam Blonde, from my local Toronto brewery. It made all the difference. I'm on top of the world. This was my shot to represent my country.' The race was not without controversy, however, as Nielsen was disqualified for having more than the allowable limit of dregs in his discarded beers. It was a schoolboy error, although under strict American liquor laws, not one that a schoolboy is allowed to make. Nielsen's misfortune also handed the team prize to Canada. Another favourite to bite the dust was Australian Josh Harris, who incurred a one-lap penalty for vomiting at the start of lap three, a mishap labelled the 'Chunder from Down Under'.

By the summer of 2016, Canadian Corey Bellemore had lowered the world record to an impressive 4:34.35 at that year's Beer Mile World Classic in London. His beer of choice was Indian brew Kingfisher. In just a few years, the sport has grown from boozy student pastime to the stage where races often attract serious athletes and hundreds of spectators. Even if you don't like beer, there are variations with vodka or whisky. Indeed, some say that the vodka two-mile gives a whole new meaning to the term 'Olympic spirit'.

BIBURY DUCK RACE, BIBURY, GLOUCESTERSHIRE, ENGLAND

Boxing Day is traditionally a day for classic sporting events, and just as the King George VI Chase at Kempton Park showcases the most talented National Hunt racehorses in the land, so the Bibury Duck Race offers spectators the chance to witness at close quarters the finest thoroughbred plastic ducks.

Every year at around 11 a.m. on Boxing Day, the Gloucestershire village of Bibury, once described by William Morris as 'the most beautiful village in England', is swamped by hordes of spectators who have finally peeled themselves off the sofa, hidden the Christmas Chocolate Orange in a safe place and come to watch thousands of plastic ducks float down the fast-flowing River Coln for two exciting races. The event is currently organised by the village cricket club, but its precise origins are shrouded in mystery. All that is known is that it dates back at least twenty-five years. The participants in the first race are 150 decoy ducks, sponsored by onlookers for £10 a head. The person whose duck crosses the finish line first nominates which charity the race proceeds should go to. The second race features more than two thousand yellow plastic ducks (the sort that children and Bill Oddie may have in their bath), with spectators able to sponsor these for just £1 each. Prizes, which sometimes include dinner for four, bottles of champagne, and even an oven-ready, non-plastic duck, are awarded to the first twenty ducks and the very last duck to finish.

The main race begins when the yellow ducks are tipped into the river by starters standing on the bridge in the centre of the village. A large net catches them at the finishing line but, don't worry, no plastic ducks are harmed in the running of the race. The ducks are then cleaned up ready for re-use the following year. However, spare a thought for the real ducks on the river. Seeing the flotilla of lifelike decoy birds relentlessly making their way downstream must produce a feeling similar to that experienced by Sir Francis Drake on spotting the Spanish Armada. Instead of engaging in battle, these latter-day drakes usually take to the skies. Race marshals, knee-deep in waders, are also on hand to prevent fowl play and assist any real ducks that are too confused by the imposters.

In 2012, the yellow duck race had to be cancelled because, following weeks of heavy rain, the Coln was at its highest recorded level ever. There were fears that hundreds of plastic ducks would jam what little space remained under the village bridge and cause the river to overflow into nearby cottages.

Whereas once upon a time plastic ducks did little more than wait to be hooked on fairground stalls, now there are similar annual races all over the world, including the **Rubber Duck Regatta** in Cincinnati, Ohio, Colorado's **Aspen Ducky Derby**, the **Great Knoxville Rubber Duck Race** in Tennessee, Australia's **Great Brisbane Duck Race**, the **Stockbridge Duck Race** in Edinburgh, Scotland, and the **Hebden Bridge Duck Race** in West Yorkshire. Meanwhile, a world record 205,000 blue rubber ducks took part in the 2009 **Great British Duck Race**, staged along a one-kilometre stretch of the River Thames near Hampton Court Palace. All of this is good news for an often-overlooked section of business enterprise. Forget about smartphones and hair extensions; the manufacture of novelty plastic ducks is surely one of the boom industries of the twenty-first century.

BRITISH LAWNMOWER RACING ASSOCIATION 12-HOUR ENDURANCE RACE, FIVE OAKS, WEST SUSSEX, ENGLAND

Motor sport is an expensive pastime for the amateur. So it was that one evening in 1973 a group of enthusiasts came to discuss the escalating costs of their favourite hobby over a pint or several at the Cricketers Arms in the West Sussex village of Wisborough Green. Among their number was Irishman Jim Gavin, who was heavily involved in rallying at the time but wanted to create a new sport that was accessible to everyone. As the beer flowed, the group's thoughts turned to alternative forms of motor sport that might be fun and cheap to run. After discarding motorised bar stools and wheelbarrows, they looked out across the village green and saw the groundsman mowing the cricket pitch. That was their Eureka moment. They all had lawnmowers in their sheds, so why not race them? This was motor sport at grass-roots level.

The first British Grand Prix meeting for lawnmowers was staged later that year at Wisborough Green. Thirty-five men went to mow, including the proud owner of a 1923 vintage motor mower. Races were divided then, as now, into three classifications: Class 1 for run-behind mowers; Class 2 for towed seat mowers with grass boxes; and Class 3, the most popular, for sit-on mowers. Classes 2 and 3 are the fastest, the latter occasionally hitting 50mph, whereas the speed of the run-behind mowers is governed solely by the ability of the perspiring runner to stay with the machine. Class 1 relay races are particularly entertaining when the drivers try to swap without losing speed or control of the mower. For safety reasons, all blades of racing mowers are removed beforehand, but otherwise only minor modifications are permitted.

The burgeoning sport received a mighty boost in 1975 from no less a figure than Sir Stirling Moss, who, attracted by the camaraderie, made his first return to motor sport since his near-fatal crash at Goodwood in 1962. Moss duly won the 1975 British Grand Prix for lawnmowers (a feat he repeated the following year), and by the end of the decade more than a hundred enthusiasts kept mowers purely for racing.

The British Lawnmower Racing Association has been formed to govern the sport, and today it runs a number of meetings between May and October, including the World Championships and the British Grand Prix. But the flagship event is the 12-Hour Endurance Race, staged at Five Oaks, just a few miles from the sport's West Sussex birthplace. First held in 1978, it takes its inspiration from the famous Le Mans 24-Hour Race, with drivers running to their machines at the start and teams of three taking it in turns to drive through the night from 8 p.m. to 8 a.m. This is Le Mans with a cutting edge. With no suspension other than a padded seat and with simple hay bales serving as crash barriers, it is no stroll in the park for the sit-on drivers as they race around the 0.9-mile field circuit at an average speed of 30mph. Past winners include five-time Le Mans champion Derek Bell, who has won the 12-Hour Lawnmower Race twice, once with Sir Stirling Moss as his co-driver. In more recent years, motorcycle ace Guy Martin has graced the event. Actor Oliver Reed, who lived nearby, regularly entered a team, which must have been a harrowing prospect for his fellow competitors, given his legendary fondness for alcohol. If you have ever seen a runaway mower demolish a garden shed and rampage through an herbaceous border, you will be aware of its capacity for destruction.

Lawnmower racing now has associations in Europe, New Zealand and the United States, where the showpiece event is the

Twelve Mile 500, a fifteen-mile, sixty-lap race held in Twelve Mile, Indiana. But for the drama of a true endurance event, the place to be is West Sussex in early August, when it's Ready, Steady, Mow!

CHEESE ROLLING, COOPER'S HILL, BROCKWORTH, GLOUCESTERSHIRE, ENGLAND

An alien visitor to Earth in 2017 might, on returning to the mother ship, be able to convince his fellow Martians that Donald Trump is now President of the United States, even that Keith Richards is still alive, but he would never be able to persuade them that there is a place in England where every year dozens of people voluntarily risk life and limb by hurling themselves down a steep hill in pursuit of a large cheese – all in the name of sport. It sounds – and is – crazy, but on the other hand, if greyhounds still think it's a good idea to chase a mechanised piece of rag around a racetrack time and time again, why shouldn't energetic country folk put their bodies on the line for a nine-pound wheel of Double Gloucester? At least the cheese is edible.

Cheese rolling in this otherwise tranquil area of rural Gloucestershire dates back to at least the fifteenth century. It is thought to have originated from a pagan ceremony in which bundles of burning brushwood were rolled down the hill to herald the advent of spring. These days, it takes place on the Spring Bank Holiday Monday at the end of May on the one-in-three gradient of Cooper's Hill. Each of the four races (three for men and one for women) begins with the wheel of cheese being released from the top of the hill, followed a second later by the runners. Strictly speaking, the aim is to catch the cheese before it reaches the bottom of the hill, but because it can hit speeds of 70mph on its descent, the cheese is rarely captured. Instead the first person to make it to the foot of the hill wins the race and the cheese. Although the runners set off in a standing position, the slope is so steep that it is virtually impossible for them to remain upright for more than a few strides and the race becomes an exercise in who can bounce down the hill the fastest. An Australian observer succinctly described the event as 'twenty young men chasing a cheese off a cliff and tumbling 200 yards to the bottom, where they are scraped up by paramedics and packed off to hospital'.

Injuries are certainly not uncommon. In 1997, thirty-three people were injured while pursuing the cheese, and in 2005 the later races were delayed as ambulances delivered victims to the local hospital before returning to wait for the next batch of casualties. With up to fifteen thousand spectators expected, the 2010 event was cancelled amid safety concerns for both participants and bystanders, and since then cheese rolling has continued on an unofficial basis. The sheer size of the cheese is enough to knock over anyone unfortunate enough to find themselves in its path, and in 2013 veteran cheese-maker Diana Smart, who had been supplying the cheese for the contest since 1988, was warned by police that she could be liable for prosecution in the event of any injuries. That year a foam replica cheese was substituted for the real thing but normal cheesy service was resumed in 2014. However, the number of runners in each race has been restricted to fifteen. Previously as many as forty took part, so that the downhill charge resembled a scene from *Zulu*.

As cheese was rationed during the Second World War, between 1941 and 1954 runners chased a wooden 'cheese' that contained a small piece of real cheese in the centre. Local man Stephen Gyde collected twenty cheeses between 1978 and 2006, but his record has been equalled by soldier Chris Anderson, who, by 2017, had won twenty cheeses in thirteen years, including, in 2011 and 2017, the coveted 'Triple Crown' – the winning of all three cheeses in a single year. One year he suffered a head injury but decided that he was fit enough to report for work the next day, only to be sent home early after putting a kettle in the fridge. Ironically, Anderson doesn't even like cheese.

Lest anyone be tempted to think that cheese rolling is nothing more than a parochial pursuit, one of the 2013 winners, Kenny Rackers, came all the way from the United States. He told the *Huffington Post*: 'I trained a long time for this, and travelled three or four thousand miles just for this race. I put it on my bucket list to win and that's what I did.' And he didn't even have to fly home with his leg in a plaster cast.

DARWIN BEER CAN BOAT RACE, DARWIN, AUSTRALIA

Two commodities never in short supply in Australia are sport-crazy men and empty beer cans. In 1974, as an initiative to clean up the beer can litter around the Northern Territory city of Darwin, local businessmen Lutz Frankenfeld and Paul Rice-Chapman combined the national thirst for sport and beer by devising the Darwin Beer Can Regatta, a day-long celebration where participants exhibit and race boats made from disused beer cans that have been painstakingly taped together in the hope that they might float. That inaugural regatta attracted 22,000 people, which was almost half of Darwin's population at the time, and more than sixty boats, proving so successful that it has gone on to become an annual event. The regatta features competitions for most creative vessels, flip-flop tossing (or thong tossing as it is confusingly known to the locals), tug-of-war competitions, and even a soft-drink-can boat race for that rarest of creatures, a teetotal Australian. But the sporting highlight is the Battle of Mindil, a contest that is part boat race and part naval battle.

The first beer can boats incorporated outboard motors, but in the 1980s beer companies changed their cans from steel to aluminium. Since the softer aluminium cans had a tendency to crush at speeds in excess of 28 knots, it was no longer deemed safe to have powered boats. So instead the boats are now propelled by sails and paddling crews. What makes the contest all the more interesting is that the vessels are not officially tested beforehand for their seaworthiness, meaning that there is a strong likelihood that not all will make it to the finish. As the *Guardian* noted: 'The boats vary in quality. Some extremely seaworthy-looking vessels took thousands of cans and many months to build. Others could have been cobbled together that morning from the leftovers of a larger than expected Saturday night.'

All entrants must conform to the Ten Can-mandments, which include: 'Thou shalt enter the event in the right spirit', 'Thou shalt build the craft of cans', 'The craft shall float by cans alone', and 'Thou shalt not drown'. At the sound of the start horn, the homemade vessels – some up to thirty feet long – head off out to sea aiming for the floating buoys that indicate the location of submerged treasure. To claim victory and the $500 in prize money, the booty has to be captured and returned ashore to the organisers' tent without being pirated. This is no easy matter as crew members pelt the opposition with flour bombs, water pistols and water balloons, and attempt to board rival boats in search of the treasure. Consequently, it is by no means certain that the first boat to reach and collect the booty will end up being declared the winner.

Organised by the Lions Club of Darwin, the regatta is held every July, one of the few times in the year when it is safe to enter the sea off Mindil Beach without fear of being stung by venomous box jellyfish. That means there are only hungry saltwater crocodiles to watch out for. The University Boat Race between Oxford and Cambridge may not be as innovative, as colourful or as boisterous as the Darwin Beer Can Race, but at least the crews do not feel obliged to carry crocodile repellent between Putney and Mortlake.

Another showcase for exotic homemade craft is the splendidly named **Float Your Fanny Down the Ganny** race in Port Hope, Ontario. The race commemorates the 1980 flood that devastated the Canadian town, the 'fannies' being the diverse, colourful boats in which competitors attempt to paddle down the 'Ganny' – the treacherous Ganaraska River.

EMMA CRAWFORD COFFIN RACES, MANITOU SPRINGS, COLORADO, USA

Around 1889, a young woman named Emma Crawford moved with her mother from Massachusetts to Manitou Springs in the hope that the local mineral springs would cure her tuberculosis. Alas, two years later Emma died at the age of twenty-eight and, in accordance with her wishes, was buried on the 7,200-foot-high summit of Red Mountain, a beauty spot overlooking the town. However, the building of a new mountain incline railway soon forced her body to be moved to a slope on the side of the peak. Then, in 1929, following several years of heavy rain, she was dislodged from her precarious perch and her remains were washed down into the canyon below, where a group of boys made a grim discovery. Only the handles of her coffin, a nameplate and a few bones were found. Although what was left of her was reburied in the town, her ghost is said to haunt Red Mountain to this day and her story became the stuff of legend.

Fast forward to 1995 when the town, looking for ideas to attract visitors, decided to put the 'fun' into funeral by staging the first Emma Crawford Coffin Race. Emma – albeit unwittingly – came racing down the mountain, they reasoned. Why not have a race in her honour? Thus, every October on the Saturday before Halloween, as many as seventy teams of five – comprising an 'Emma' in a coffin-like contraption on wheels pushed by four 'mourners' – speed along a 195-yard course through the centre of Manitou Springs. The teams compete against each other in pairs in a series of heats, the fastest overall time being declared the eventual winner. Ties may or may not be described as 'dead heats'.

Naturally everyone has to look the part and team members dress up as pirates, ghouls, Smurfs and even zombie transvestite nurses. Meanwhile the homemade coffins are decked out to look like everything from a baby's pram to the Popemobile. The racing Emmas must all be aged eighteen or over, so nobody can get away with pushing a lightweight child. They must also wear helmets, not least because statistics show that the mortality rate is quite high among occupants of coffins. Competition rules point out that at least three of the four runners must be in direct contact with the coffin at all times during the race, otherwise the coffin will be deemed to be out of control and will be disqualified. And, let's be honest, nobody wants a runaway coffin. Those in the know say the key to success is to build an aerodynamic coffin and to make sure that your Emma lies as prone as possible in order to reduce wind resistance. Prior to the races there is a grand coffin parade, featuring the competitors' ingenious creations as well as elaborate real hearses driven by members of the Denver Hearse Association. Prizes are awarded for Best Coffin, Best Emma and Best Entourage. The event draws more than ten thousand spectators to the town each year, so despite the fact that Emma Crawford is long dead, she lives on in the healthy ker-ching of tourism.

EMPIRE STATE BUILDING RUN-UP, NEW YORK CITY, USA

There is a perfectly good lift that takes visitors to the observatory on the eighty-sixth floor of the Empire State Building in under a minute. Yet since 1978, thousands of intrepid souls have instead insisted on running up the stairs – all 1,576 of them: a climb that takes over ten times longer. Madness doesn't begin to cover it.

As you might expect from an event that incorporates a vertical climb of around one fifth of a mile, this is a race for serious athletes. If your only prior training is once having gone up the stairs at home two at a time because you were caught short en route to the bathroom, give it a miss. As the world's 'marquee tower climb', it attracts elite runners from across the globe, and these start from the lobby at the head of the field, with the rest following on at short staggered intervals to avoid an almighty pile-up with everyone trying to get into the stairwell at the same time. Whereas climbing the stairs of a standard apartment block would require negotiating the occasional abandoned supermarket trolley or prone drunk, the Empire State Building stairs are mercifully kept free of obstruction. Also, unlike the modern marathon, there is rarely a fancy-dress element, so competitors do not run the risk of being wedged in the narrow stairwell by someone wheezing away inside a King Kong costume.

Americans Gary Muhrcke and Marcy Schwam won the very first Empire State Building Run-Up, and it was not until 1995 that a non-American, Germany's Kurt König, emerged triumphant. The first non-American to win the women's event was Australian Angela Sheean in 1999. The men's record of 9:33 was set by Australia's Paul Crake while notching his fifth consecutive victory in 2003, and the fastest woman to complete the climb was Andrea Mayr of Austria in 11:23 in 2006 (her third straight win). Germany's

Thomas Dold won the race for an unprecedented seven years in a row between 2006 and 2012, while in 2017 Australia's Suzy Walsham chalked up her eighth win in the women's race. Construction work meant that from 1991 to 1994, the race finished on the eightieth floor.

Over six hundred runners take part every February, including many who do so for charitable causes. The 2017 field included Roseann Sdoia, who lost part of her leg in the Boston Marathon bombing. It is a tough climb, but some of the non-elite runners save their legs by using the handrails to pull themselves up. With a basic level of fitness, you should expect to reach the top in around half an hour. Stair master Brian Kuritzky advises would-be competitors to train for the event by finding a tall building and running up 30,000 stairs. As for the race itself, he told the *New York Daily News*: 'It's emotionally draining because you are grinding from flight to flight and not seeing anything other than the white stone stairs. But by breaking the eighty-six flights into sets of ten, you can set small, attainable goals that will take you to the top.' Or you could take the lift.

GREAT KLONDIKE INTERNATIONAL OUTHOUSE RACE, DAWSON CITY, YUKON, CANADA

If modern man's refuge from the stress of family life is his garden shed, back in the days of the Klondike Gold Rush in the 1890s, it was his outhouse, or outside toilet. It was a place where he could go to contemplate the meaning of life, to sit in blissful solitude and near-silence, and, just occasionally, to wonder why his wife, for all her undoubted virtues, had neglected to replenish the pile of toilet paper. The outhouse was very much a symbol of life in North America and, in some more remote areas, remains so to this day. Nobody seems quite sure how this iconic architectural feature first became the foundation for a madcap race around Dawson City in 1977, but it seems certain that drink was somehow involved.

In the early years, it was quite a haphazard affair, with some racers stopping off at various bars along the route, where they became so refreshed that they didn't bother continuing to the finish. So a time limit was introduced, and now, as one observer put it, the outhouses 'charge through the streets of Dawson like a dose of castor oil'.

Teams are composed of five people, all aged sixteen or over, one of whom must be seated on the toilet at all times. Although decorated for the occasion, the contraptions must look as much like outhouses as possible – with the exception of a functioning plumbing system. Only the runners can propel the wheeled outhouses, usually with the aid of rickshaw-like bars. No mechanisms or motors are allowed. For those unable to build their own, metal outhouses are available for hire for the day.

Among the more memorable designs have been the Elton John, the Royal Flush, Dumped at the Altar, and a bizarre airplane-like outhouse, complete with propellers and a twenty-foot wingspan that nearly caused havoc with parked cars' wing mirrors as it turned corners. In 1986, a group of Anglican ministers, who were in Dawson for an ordination, entered the race and transformed their privy into a devouthouse. On that basis, be prepared for entries from a team of traffic cops (the over and outhouse), defence lawyers (the beyond reasonable doubthouse) and Lulu impersonators (the you make me wanna shouthouse).

As befits its grandiose title, the race, held on Labour Day Sunday at the start of September, is now a truly international event, with teams coming from as far afield as Europe and Alaska. The old course measured 1.86 miles, and so runners used to take turns in sitting on the throne to give their team-mates a short rest. However, in recent years it has sometimes been shortened in distance with the addition of a dastardly obstacle course near the finish. So a team may lead all the way round, only to fall at the final hurdle and, like Napoleon, meet their Portaloo.

GREAT KNARESBOROUGH BED RACE,
KNARESBOROUGH, NORTH YORKSHIRE, ENGLAND

Back in June 1966, the newly formed Knaresborough Round Table was looking to set up a regular charity fundraising event. It could have taken the form of a soapbox derby, a raft race on the River Nidd or a tug-of-war contest, but instead the organisers settled on a manic bed race along a 2.4-mile course through the historic town's picturesque but often near-perpendicular streets, incorporating a desperate twenty-yard swim across the fast-flowing river shortly before the finish line. Just four teams competed in that inaugural time trial, but the event has now become so well established in the Yorkshire sporting calendar that half a century later ninety teams of seven take part – six bed-pushers (or runners) and one 'sleeper', who is obliged to remain on the bed at all times. If you think the latter is the easy option, try sitting in a bed on wheels when it is propelled at speed across the cobbled stones of the Marketplace. Suffice to say that in the aftermath of the race Knaresborough's dentists are kept busy.

To reduce the risk of injury in the contest that put the 'bed' into 'bedlam', all sleepers must wear helmets and, with a view to the river crossing, lifejackets. The race rules also stipulate that each bed must have a built-in buoyancy aid capable of supporting bed and passenger for up to five minutes, adding ominously that the bed must have 'an aperture large enough to allow the passenger to escape quickly if required'. Just in case, divers are on hand to pluck team members from the Nidd's icy waters. It may be June, but June in Yorkshire merely means that only one layer of thermals is required.

Race day begins at Knaresborough Castle with a competition for the best-dressed bed. Each year, the organisers (in 1999,

Knaresborough Lions took over from the Round Table) come up with a different theme, such as Nursery Rhymes, Olympic Nations, Myths and Legends or Film Characters. The best-dressed bed then leads a parade of the teams, with all participants in fancy dress, through the town to Conyngham Hall. There, the beds are stripped of their decorations in readiness for the race itself. With 630 people involved, if they all set off at the same time the result would be a carnage not witnessed in the town since Oliver Cromwell's troops stormed the Royalist stronghold in 1644. So they start at ten-second intervals, with the likely victors (based on general fitness and previous performance) going first. The team with the fastest time is declared the winner. Apart from one almost vertical drop that has been declared too dangerous to navigate, the course has remained largely unchanged since 1966. It features steep climbs and descents, a stretch across rough parkland and the final epic swim. On two occasions – in 1972 and 1998 – the river crossing had to be scrapped because heavy rain had caused the river to swell to flood level, but the event has never been cancelled. The winning teams expect to complete the course in around fourteen minutes.

The very first Knaresborough Bed Race was won by the Army Apprentices College team from nearby Harrogate, but only because the US Army team from Menwith Hill made the mistake of entering the river several hundred yards before they needed to and thus dropped from first to last place. In 1995, the prefix 'Great' was added to the event to distinguish it from other bed races that it had spawned in Germany and the USA. The German event was first staged in Knaresborough's twin town of Bebra in the early 1980s under the name of *Sanftenrennen*, with the all-conquering ICI team nobly pushing their bed 500 miles from Yorkshire to Bebra in order to take part. Bed-pushers don't come any more dedicated than that.

HENLEY-ON-TODD RIVER RACE, ALICE SPRINGS, AUSTRALIA

Just as England has the social splendour of the Henley Royal Regatta, with its straw boaters, striped blazers and jugs of Pimm's, so Australia stages a rival occasion – the annual Henley-on-Todd Regatta, with corked hats, sweaty vests and cans of beer. There is one other key difference between the two sporting events: unlike the Thames, Australia's Todd River, located in the heart of the arid Outback, is dry. So instead of rowing along the course, Australian teams run barefoot carrying bottomless boats along the hot sandy riverbed, operating on the same scientific principle as Fred Flintstone's car.

The idea for a gathering that gently mocked the English was the brainchild of Alice Springs Meteorological Bureau officer Reg Smith who, during a Rotary Club picnic in 1962, proposed that the town should stage its own version of the Henley Regatta, apparently undeterred by the fact it was nearly 1,000 miles from the nearest sizeable body of water. 'Okay, what about the boats?' asked a fellow Rotarian. 'Do we tow them or push them?' 'Neither,' replied Reg. 'We cut the bottoms out and carry them!'

The inaugural Henley-on-Todd Regatta – or Todd River Race as it is sometimes known – was staged in December 1962 but it has since moved to the third Saturday in August. With a history of over fifty years, it is the longest-running event in the Northern Territory. As well as the traditional dry rowing races for fours and eights, there is a dry kayak race for solo competitors, plus a yacht race, where bottomless yachts are carried by crews of four or six. The great advantage of dry yacht racing is that the crews don't have to worry about winds or currents and there is certainly no need for all of that jibing and tacking nonsense. Lifejackets are also considered surplus to requirement. The aforementioned craft are all supplied by the organisers but there is also a series of 'Bring Your Own Boat' races for four-member crews who wish to run along carrying lightweight boats of their own design. If you were still in any doubt as to whether or not the event is supposed to be taken seriously, 'No Fishing' signs are posted along the river.

As the world's only dry river regatta, Henley-on-Todd is also the only regatta to have been cancelled because there was water in the river. That happened in 1993 when unexpected rainfall in the area actually caused the River Todd to flow.

ISU-1 OFFICE CHAIR GRAND PRIX, KYOTANABE, JAPAN

The Isu-1 (Chair-1) Grand Prix is a relatively new addition to the world sports calendar. First raced in 2010, it sees competitors wheel themselves around a tight, twisty 180-metre-long course on the streets of Kyotanabe for two hours while riding ordinary office chairs. It is very much an endurance test, with participants competing in teams of three who take it in turns to occupy the hot seat. The winning team is the one that completes the most laps in the two hours.

The event was founded by photographic shop owner Tsuyoshi Tahara after he and other small businesses around the Kirara shopping arcade found themselves struggling in the face of competition from the high-end malls that had opened up in the area. Most businessmen in a similar situation might have distributed flyers or taken out advertising, but for some reason best known to himself, Tahara thought the best way to attract attention was to stage an office-chair marathon. Those who scoffed at the idea were soon left with sushi on their face as the chair race became so popular that it is now held every March and has led to similar contests in a dozen other Japanese prefectures. In 2015, Tahara and other organisers set up an official Japan Office Race Chair Association. He told japanbullet.com: 'We all remember being scolded for driving chairs when we were kids, but this race gives a liberating feeling for all participants by allowing them to ride the chairs just how they like.'

The Kyotanabe street circuit's tight hairpin bends mean that riders need strong thighs and even tougher footwear. They wear helmets and knee and elbow pads as spills are numerous and the concrete surface is unforgiving. Little quarter is given, especially when cornering, with race tactics sometimes appearing to owe more to bumper cars than F1. Just to add to the risk factor, the fastest speeds are achieved by riding the chairs backwards, which means that competitors are constantly looking over their shoulders to see where they are going. One lapse of concentration and it is easy to end up in a shop front with your wheels in the air.

Chairs must not be modified, apart from decorations, and teams can prepare a spare chair if the original is destroyed during the race. This is a wise precaution because the chairs, particularly the armrests and backrests, do have a tendency to break, which is not unreasonable considering that they were only designed for short scoots to the stationery cabinet for those too lazy to get up and walk to the nest of paper clips, and not for flying around the street for two hours in the hands of a bunch of lunatics.

Around sixty teams take part each year, and the winners can expect to complete around a hundred and thirty laps in the two hours – about a lap per minute. While most riders opt for stretchy sportswear, it is refreshing to note that a few pay homage to their mode of transport's natural habitat by wearing shirt and tie. As a reward for their effort and entertainment value, the winning team is presented with 90 kilos of rice.

Not only has the race boosted business in the Kirara arcade, it has also served as an invaluable promotional tool for Osaka-based office supplier Kokuyo, who have entered a team every year. 'It is the best opportunity to let people know the durability of our office chairs,' said a company official. Certainly if they can withstand 100-plus laps around the streets of Kyotanabe, they can be expected to support the average middle manager in meaningless meetings for years.

MAN VERSUS HORSE MARATHON,
LLANWRTYD WELLS, POWYS, WALES

Like so many of the more eccentric sporting challenges, the idea for a marathon race between humans and horses was born in a pub. In 1980, Gordon Green, landlord of the Neuadd Arms in the Welsh town of Llanwrtyd Wells, overheard a discussion between two of his customers. One claimed that over a significant distance across country, a man was equal to any horse. Green decided that the only way to settle the argument was to hold such a race in full public view, and so the Man Versus Horse Marathon was staged over a twenty-two-mile course – slightly shorter than a traditional marathon, but on rougher terrain incorporating steep hills, rocky descents, energy-sapping bogs and hazardous river crossings. Humans start fifteen minutes ahead of the horses and their riders, meaning that as well as having to cover the ground as quickly as possible, runners also face the prospect of periodically having to throw themselves into a hedge or a ditch to avoid being trampled underhoof. It is not a handicap race, but the organisers thought that the presence of hundreds of runners en masse at the start would scare the horses, and so man and beast set off separately with the fifteen minutes deducted from the horses' finishing times.

That first marathon was comfortably won by horse and rider, a trend that continued for twenty-four years until 2004 when British athlete Huw Lobb beat the first horse home by over two minutes. In doing so, he collected a prize of £25,000, which had accumulated by £1,000 each year from the race's inception until it was claimed by a winning runner. Bookmakers also had to pay out on scores of bets struck at sixteen to one. The temperature for the 2004 race was higher than normal, and this is thought to have contributed to the historic result, as horses overheat quickly. Nor are they as adept as humans at making steep descents – another area where the runners can hope to sneak an advantage. Lobb told the BBC: 'As an experienced fell runner I was climbing up steep banks, jumping off ledges and throwing myself down steep hills in a way no horse could ever hope to do. So while a horse is definitely faster over the flat, I'd say only about 20 per cent of the course I ran was on flat ground.'

That year, no fewer than 500 runners and 40 horses took part in the challenge. Three years later, Germany's Florian Holzinger repeated the feat, beating the equine field by close to eleven minutes. Otherwise horses have reigned supreme. Lobb tried again in 2012, but, on a cloudy, cooler day, Iola Evans on Rheidol Star beat him by almost half an hour. Lobb's cause was probably not helped by running the Cork Marathon just five days earlier.

The race takes place each year in June, and even featured cyclists between 1985 and 1992. Indeed, in 1989, British cyclist Tim Gould beat the first horse home by three minutes, but was unable to claim the main prize, which was reserved for runners. The Welsh government subsequently banned cyclists from taking part, arguing that their wheels damaged forest paths. The 2009 race was marred by controversy when, in addition to the fifteen-minute start, the organisers decided to deduct time spent in the halfway-point vet checks from the horses' times. This enabled horse to beat human by eight minutes, but created such bad feeling that the fastest runner, Martin Cox, refused to accept his trophy in protest. Harmony was restored the following year when the additional deduction was scrapped. The 2013 race attracted a record entry of sixty-five horses, with forty-four completing the course, enabling it to lay claim to being the world's largest horse race and almost certainly the world's only marathon where four legs compete against two.

PANCAKE RACE, OLNEY, BUCKINGHAMSHIRE, ENGLAND

In one respect the annual pancake race at Olney is the most keenly contested sporting event in England, because it is the one race where everyone gives a toss.

The story goes that back in 1445 an Olney housewife was making pancakes when she suddenly heard the bells summoning her to church. Horrified at the prospect of missing the Shriving service, at which she could confess her sins on the day before the start of Lent, she hurried along the road with frying pan still in hand, tossing the pancake as she ran to prevent it from burning. To commemorate her frantic dash, the local townswomen instigated a pancake race, which has been passed on from generation to generation for nearly 600 years. Although the race lapsed during the Second World War, it was revived shortly afterwards and once again takes place every year at five minutes before noon on Shrove Tuesday.

All the women in the race wear apron and headscarf in memory of the original Olney runner and must toss their pancakes at both the start and the finish of the 415-yard course, which runs through the centre of town from the marketplace to the Church of St Peter and St Paul. The twenty-five participants need to be over the age of eighteen and must have lived in Olney for at least three months, which is one way of ensuring that an outsider never wins. The sprint gets underway when the starter announces, 'Toss your pancakes', and rings a hand bell. Competitors often range in age from eighteen to eighty, and the 2016 race saw Lianne Fisher set a new course record of 55.02 seconds. Among the most successful pancake racers of recent years is Devon Byrne, a three-time winner. Following her 2014 success, she revealed to ITV: 'My mum won the race three times in the 1990s. The last time she won, she was pregnant with me, so I guess it is in my blood.' Few would dispute that it is better to have pancakes in your blood than blood in your pancakes.

The traditional prize for the winner is a kiss from the verger, but if that wasn't excitement enough, since 1950 Olney has competed against the women from Liberal, Kansas, for the International Pancake Race. Liberal was inspired to hold its own event after seeing pictures of the Olney race. Each town runs its race over the same distance, on the same day and at a similar hour (in terms of local time), and the fastest time from the two is declared the outright winner. After 2017, the score stood at 37–29 in favour of Liberal with no-contests declared in 2017 because of a timer glitch and in 1980 because a clumsily parked BBC Television van blocked the finish line in Olney. There are times when you can simply have too much media attention.

PIG-N-FORD RACES, TILLAMOOK, OREGON, USA

Since 1925, the Tillamook County Fair, held annually in Oregon in August, has staged a curious event in which drivers race around a dirt track at the wheel of a stripped-down Model T Ford while carrying a live pig under one arm. If you can imagine Sebastian Vettel speeding around Monaco with one hand on the steering wheel while carrying 20 pounds of wriggling, squealing bacon under his other arm, you'll pretty much get the picture.

The concept has its roots in the early 1920s when a local man driving a Model T Ford saw a neighbour's pig running loose, chased it down in the car and scooped it up. The story captured people's imaginations to such an extent that they decided to turn it into an annual event.

Following a series of elimination heats, five cars take part in the final and line up on the start line with their engines off. The drivers stand next to the grandstands, and when the starting pistol is fired, they sprint across to the pig pens, grab a young pig, hand-crank their car and set off around the track. At the end of the lap, they stop, turn off the engine, pick up a different pig, and race another lap. The first driver to complete three laps in this manner – without losing their pig – is declared the winner. The average winning time is a little over a minute per lap. The victorious driver receives a trophy; the victorious pigs go away only with memories.

If the modern race sounds chaotic, think what it must have been like in the old days when the drivers used to wrestle 90-pound adult pigs to their cars, the animals' rear hooves dragging in the dirt.

Technique is key, particularly when deciding whether to hold the pig face up or face down in the car. 'They like to poop a lot,' warned driver John Haertel in an interview with the *Wall Street Journal*, 'so you get some of that on your car. They feed them pretty good.' Haertel practises with a slick-sided jug filled with rocks. 'If I can hold on to that, then I'm definitely going to make sure that I can hold on to a pig.' Everybody concerned is at pains to point out that the pigs are treated humanely and are always handled in a way that is good for the driver and good for the pig. It does help if you can find a relatively relaxed animal. Before selecting his pig from the pen, fellow driver Marty Walker quickly pokes them and grabs 'whichever one doesn't freak out'.

Walker is very much the Lewis Hamilton of Pig-N-Ford racing. He has hogged the limelight since the 1990s, racking up over a dozen wins, although he was sensationally disqualified in 2010 in what became known as the Great Camshaft Controversy. Walker's rivals suspected that he had cheated on the way to what was then his ninth win, so they exercised their rights under Article 7 of the Tillamook County Model T Pig and Ford Association rules, which lets members pay $100 to challenge a vehicle's legality. Those regulations prohibit any souping up of the basic engine – you can't change the torque for the pork – but Walker's challengers found that his engine had an altered camshaft, which can increase power. Consequently he was stripped of his 2010 title and the event was forced to adopt stringent, NASCAR-style standards. This includes stopping drivers deliberately bumping into each other on the run to the pen or during the mayhem of the pig exchange. In Pig-N-Ford, there is no room for boorish behaviour.

PUMPKIN KAYAKING, WINDSOR, NOVA SCOTIA, CANADA

There are various uses for a hollowed-out pumpkin – Halloween decoration, avant-garde table lamp, emergency crash helmet, to name just three – but few would consider its benefits as a mode of transport. Canada's annual Windsor Pumpkin Regatta aims to correct that oversight by encouraging competitors to race pumpkins over a half-mile course across Lake Pesaquid (sometimes spelt Pisiquid). There are three classes – paddling (which is the most popular), motorised (where an outboard motor is attached to the pumpkin), and experimental (where just about anything goes). The racing pumpkins are known as PVC (personal vegetable craft), even though the pumpkin is technically a fruit.

The key to success in pumpkin racing lies in the preparation. First, you need a pumpkin large enough to seat at least one adult, as entrants can be either soloists or pairs. Most of the racing pumpkins weigh in excess of 600 pounds and some reach as much as 12 feet in circumference. The pumpkin then needs to be hollowed out using a flesh scooper, but this task can only be performed a few days before the race, or it will turn soft and lose its buoyancy. Finally, the exterior of the pumpkin is painted with a colourful design and a name, with the paddler wearing a costume to match. 'Racers must be physically fit,' warns an expert in the field, 'for a pumpkin doesn't easily glide through the water. Large, round objects aren't the most co-operative vessels.'

The regatta, which takes place each October, was founded in 1999 by Danny Dill, the son of Howard Dill, whose main claim to fame was that he bred the formidable Atlantic Giant, a veritable colossus of a pumpkin. In the race's infancy, Leo Swinamer proved the pumpkin kayaker to beat, winning the paddling class for the first nine years, his last victory in 2007 being at the ripe old age of seventy-three. He has also won the motorised category. Despite his dominance, the contest continued to grow in popularity and when his run was ended in 2008 by his nephew Anthony Cook, who had decorated his huge half-pumpkin to resemble a football, more than ten thousand spectators turned up to watch sixty racers. Swinamer had hoped to make it ten in a row that year but was sensationally disqualified when his pumpkin sank during the qualifying event. His elimination shook the pumpkin sporting world to the core. Cook triumphed again in 2015, pushing his aged uncle, who had come out of retirement for one last shot at the title, into second place.

Unlike conventional canoeing or kayaking, pumpkin racing can be affected by a bad harvest. A prolonged drought in 2016 resulted in smaller-than-usual pumpkins for that year's regatta, meaning that there were more solo competitors than pairs. The winning kayaker usually takes around twenty minutes to cross the lake. The 2011 and 2014 champion, local headmaster Joe Seagram, emphasised the problems inherent in controlling and steering a pumpkin. 'Imagine getting into a giant teacup,' he told CBC News, 'it's tippy and 360 degrees, and it'll spin, so if you're paddling to the right, it'll spin to the left; paddle to the left, it'll spin to the right.' Gourd does indeed move in mysterious ways.

The appeal of the event was summed up by 2015 entrant Beverley Marier. 'What's more fabulous than getting in a giant piece of fruit and calling it a boat? As soon as I saw it, I knew I had to. How many people can say they rode in a giant pumpkin?' Around Windsor, Nova Scotia, quite a few.

RACE THE TRAIN, TYWYN, GWYNEDD, WALES

In many regions of twenty-first-century Britain, the biggest challenge with arranging a running race against a train is actually finding a train to race. However, the historic Talyllyn Railway in Mid-Wales is a preserved narrow-gauge railway run largely by volunteers and enthusiasts and, as such, its trains are not prone to wholesale cancellations because of industrial action, leaves on the line or the wrong kind of snow. The fact that its steam locomotives trundle along at a gentle average speed of 9mph to take in the breathtaking Welsh countryside also makes them an ideal opponent for cross-country runners.

The idea of local dentist Godfrey Worsey and organised by the Tywyn Rotary Club every August, the race was first run in 1984 with a field of just under fifty runners, but the following year that number had increased to 250 and today the event attracts over 1,000 competitors. The fourteen-mile course runs roughly parallel to the railway track from Tywyn to Abergynolwyn and back, taking the athletes along footpaths and roads, up hill and down dale, and across farmland. There are thrills and the occasional spills, which may leave runners, like steam locomotives, with a tender behind. Although there are ten stations en route in each direction, only the elite runners – about 10 per cent of the field – manage to stay ahead of the train for the full distance. Spectators can book their seat on the train, thus allowing them the opportunity to hurl encouragement or abuse at the runners without having to get off their backsides.

Runners and the ninety-year-old engine set off simultaneously from Tywyn at the sound of the train whistle and the train's timetable schedules it to complete the round trip in one hour and forty-seven minutes. Athletes come all the way from New Zealand,

Australia and the United States, seeking to win the race, record a personal best or, at the very least, beat the train back to Tywyn. The 2016 winner, Sale Harrier Paul Green, recorded a time of 1:28.15, beating the train by nearly twenty minutes. The men's record, set in 2008, stands at 1:18.15. The women's record is 1:34.20 set by Angela Leck in 2014, and there is a cash prize to anyone who breaks either record. To deter too many no-hopers, there is a time limit of three hours and fifteen minutes to complete the course, at which point all the official timekeepers go home. For those liable to run out of puff, a series of shorter races on the morning of the main event tackles sections of the railway from 3.5 to 6.2 miles. Again trains are involved.

Originally opened in 1866 to carry slate to Tywyn from local quarries, the Talyllyn Railway helped provide Rev. W. Awdry, who served as a volunteer guard on the line in 1952, with stories for his Thomas the Tank Engine books. Perhaps the Fat Controller could have shed a few pounds by leaving the comfort of his office and racing the train. There has never been any thought of switching the event from the Talyllyn to a main line, not least because inevitably it would sometimes have to be renamed Race the Replacement Bus Service.

RARÁJIPARI, CHIHUAHUA, MEXICO

Also known as the kickball race, rarájipari is contested by two teams of the native Tarahumara people who try to outpace each other at kicking a wooden ball across the rugged mountain landscape of north-west Mexico. In friendly, casual games, this might go on for just under seven miles, but in serious competition between rival villages, a kickball race can last two days and nights and cover distances of up to a hundred and fifty miles.

Two teams of between three and ten men take part. One member of each team takes the ball, which is approximately the size of a baseball, and kicks it ahead. The members of that team then chase after the ball, whereupon the front man kicks it again. One player is usually designated to be the front-runner, who is in charge of the ball for the first part of the race. However, after a few miles, or if there is a delay because the ball has become stuck under a boulder or rolled down a canyon, the rest of the team catches up and the front man is allowed to give his feet a rest by dropping back into the pack – rather like the team pursuit in cycling. Throughout the contest, each team focuses solely on its own ball; it is not meant to be a contact sport, and interfering with opponents or the opposing team's ball is simply not rarájipari. However, since betting on the outcome is widespread, cheating does take place. The race ends when the first team – and its ball – reaches the finish point agreed by both teams before the start.

The ideal footwear for kicking a wooden ball for hours on end would be sturdy builder's boots but these are not exactly suitable for long-distance running. You can't help feeling that Mo Farah might be less effective lapping the track in a pair of Doc Martens. So the Tarahumara run in homemade sandals or even barefoot, flicking the ball into the air with their toes in a sort of shovel kick.

Since they also choose to run on the tips of their toes, it would seem that they have built up extra resilience in that area of the foot. In long races that run overnight, spectators from the community light makeshift torches to show the way and team members sometimes wear rattles on their bodies to stay awake.

All runners are banned from having sex on the eve of the race, but, as an alternative, they smoke a mixture of tobacco and dried bats' blood, washed down with corn-based beer. Fortunately there are no random drug tests in rarájipari. Meanwhile, in the absence of a four-leafed clover or a lucky horseshoe, the rival medicine men go out and dig up the shin bones of a dead person, crush it into a fine powder and then sprinkle it across the track to bring the runners good luck during the race. They also take time to put a curse on their opponents.

The Tarahumara routinely run 100 miles a day even when they're not racing. Two members of the tribe were entered for the marathon at the 1928 Amsterdam Olympics in the hope of persuading the organisers to make a sixty-mile race an Olympic distance. The Mexican trainers neglected to mention to the pair that the marathon was still a more modest twenty-six miles, with the result that after crossing the finish line in thirty-second and thirty-fifth place, they continued running, unaware that the race was over. When officials finally caught up with them and persuaded them to stop, the Tarahumara were heard to wail: 'Too short! Too short!'

WIFE CARRYING WORLD CHAMPIONSHIPS, SONKAJÄRVI, FINLAND

According to popular Finnish legend, a nineteenth-century ne'er-do-well by the name of Herkko Rosvo-Ronkainen had a worrying tendency to emerge from his woodland home with his gang of fellow thieves, raid local villages and run off with their money and their womenfolk. Rosvo-Ronkainen and his gang of wife stealers apparently used to carry the protesting women on their backs while making their escape before eventually claiming them as their own wives. It was all highly irregular, but the tales inspired the Finns to develop the sport of wife carrying, and in 1992 the town of Sonkajärvi staged the first world championships. They have since been held annually in July.

The object of the exercise is simple – male competitors carry women along a 253.5-metre-long obstacle course, which includes a couple of fences and a pool filled with about three feet of water, in the fastest possible time. If a man drops his wife at any point, fifteen seconds is added to their time. It usually takes the winners just over a minute to complete the course. The event is run in a series of two-man heats, and the wife carrier with the quickest time overall is declared world champion and is presented with the woman's weight in beer. So although it is obviously an advantage to carry a lighter wife, your prize will not be as substantial. In any case, the rules of the contest state that all wives being carried must weigh a minimum of seven and a half stone. If you have picked up a size-zero supermodel, she will be burdened with a rucksack containing the additional weight needed to reach that figure. At this juncture it should be pointed out that the woman does not necessarily have to be the carrier's wife; she could be someone else's wife, or indeed nobody's wife, just a willing participant. However, given the close physical proximity that carrier and carried need to adopt for the occasion, it is probably best if they are at least acquainted. If not, they may well be soon afterwards. Several types of carry may be practised: piggyback, fireman's carry (over the shoulder), or Estonian-style, where the wife hangs upside down on her husband's back and hangs on to his waist with her legs clamped tightly around his head. This position, which leaves his hands free, can be found on page 128 of the Estonian version of the *Kama Sutra*.

With a view to marital harmony, the organisers advise: 'Generally the best wife is the wife of one's own, all the more if she is harmonious, gentle and able to keep her balance while riding on the shoulders of her man.' To establish a successful wife-carrying partnership, they go on to recommend a training regime that involves 'carrying your wife as part of daily routines, in the bath or in the supermarket'. Not sure how that would go down at the local Waitrose.

The stand-out couple of recent years have been Finland's Taisto Miettinen and Kristiina Haapanen, who were undefeated in the competition over a five-year period from 2009 to 2013. Miettinen, a lawyer, trains for the event by wearing ski boots to build up his leg muscles. Estonia's Margo Uusorg is also a five-time world champion, but with three different women. For a female perspective, Inga Klauso, who has twice been carried to victory by Margo Uusorg's brother Madis, admitted to BBC News: 'It's pretty unpleasant, but not as bad as it seems.' This is hardly a ringing endorsement.

Unsurprisingly, the Wife Carrying World Championships have been dominated by Finns and Estonians, but it attracts competitors from more than ten different countries, including the UK, Ireland, Japan, Germany, Israel, Russia and the United States.

Indeed, other nations of the world have been quick to seize upon its sporting potential. The **North American Wife Carrying Championships** take place every year on Columbus Day weekend in October at Newry, Maine, and the **UK Wife Carrying Championships** are held in Dorking, Surrey, in March. When the UK event was first run in 2008, it was announced as the re-introduction of wife carrying to these shores after an absence of nearly 900 years. Hong Kong has staged a similar contest on Valentine's Day, but with the added twist of the wife having to lean down and pick up roses en route. Australia has held its own national championships since 2005 in Singleton, New South Wales, and, in the spirit of equal opportunities, has also introduced a joint **Wife Carrying and Husband Dragging** contest. The men act as a dead weight and are pulled by their partners along the ground from a makeshift bar 'depicting a traditional Aussie weekend where the female drags her man out of the pub'.

WORLD CHAMPIONSHIP BATHTUB RACE, NANAIMO, BRITISH COLUMBIA, CANADA

St Andrew's is the 'Home of Golf', Cheltenham is known as the 'Home of National Hunt Racing' and Lord's is generally regarded as the 'Home of Cricket'. To that list of renowned sporting venues can be added the city of Nanaimo, British Columbia, which is acknowledged unanimously as the 'Bathtub Racing Capital of the World'.

The World Championship Bathtub Race was first held in 1967 – Canada's centenary year – partly to boost local tourism and partly to demonstrate that there was more fun to be had in a bathtub than just sinking the *Bismarck* and creating your own natural bubble bath. That inaugural event was billed as the Nanaimo to Vancouver Great International World Championship Bathtub Race and it remained part of the Vancouver Sea Festival until the festival's demise in the mid-1990s. More than two hundred tubbers took part in a wide range of tubs fitted with outboard motors and, amazingly, forty-seven managed to complete the thirty-six-mile course. The race is now held annually on the last weekend in July around a thirty-seven-mile course starting and finishing in Nanaimo. Bathtub racing owes a lot to former Nanaimo mayor Frank Ney, who not only promoted the event but was also a regular participant and seemingly enjoyed nothing more than touring the region dressed as a pirate.

Today's craft resemble typical powerboats, except that the driver is sitting in a bathtub. The roll-top tub must be an integral part of the structure even though the finished article is a streamlined fibreglass vessel and, fitted with an engine, capable of reaching speeds of over 30mph. It gives fresh meaning to the declaration: 'I'm just going for a quick bath.' Bouncing across the waves at speed for over an hour can be an uncomfortable experience, especially if a design fault has left the driver squatting at the tap end. Although the event attracts serious racers, there is also a prize for the more humble entrant, the Silver Plunger award presented to the first tub to sink. In some years, many don't even make it out of Nanaimo Harbour.

If the Nanaimo event sounds a little too hi-tech for your taste and you prefer to search for the soap at a more leisurely pace, try the good clean fun of the **World Tin Bath Championships**, which were first held in 1971 and take place on a 400-metre course around Castletown Harbour on the Isle of Man every July. It is an event for solo paddlers, and the winner is the first person to reach the finish line or the one who covers the furthest distance without sinking. In the hope of avoiding that ignominy, each tin bath is allowed one wooden outrigger and two buoyancy aids. Over a hundred inveterate bath paddlers converge on the town each year, including competitors from such far-flung spots as New Zealand, South Africa, Latvia, Ukraine and the United States. However, the one to beat is local woman Erika Cowen, who claimed her sixteenth victory in the women's race in 2015. It will come as no surprise to learn that the tin bath race is organised by the town's Ale Drinkers Society.

WORLD COAL CARRYING CHAMPIONSHIPS, GAWTHORPE, WEST YORKSHIRE

One Sunday lunchtime in 1963 at the Beehive pub in Gawthorpe, Yorkshire, Louis Hartley told fellow miner Reggie Sedgwick: 'You're looking tired.' 'I'm fitter than thee,' came the reply, at which point coal merchant Amos Clapham chipped in: 'And I'm fitter than the both of you.' This was fighting talk, and as the argument became more heated, the trio started betting on who could run furthest and fastest with a sack of coal on his back. Thus was born the World Coal Carrying Championships, where every Easter Monday competitors race 1,012 metres from the Royal Oak pub in Ossett to the finish at the maypole green in Gawthorpe. The time is recorded when the runner's sack hits the green, which, given the exhausting nature of the event, is usually just a split second before the runner. The men carry a 50-kilo sack (equal to the old imperial hundredweight or 112 pounds) and the women carry 20 kilos.

Ironically, none of the three original pub protagonists ever took part in the race. As one sage has noted: 'There are two great traditions in Gawthorpe: one is competing in a coal-carrying championship, the other is talking about competing in it.'

Plenty have taken part, however, including Yorkshireman David Jones, whose winning time of four minutes six seconds in 1991 and again in 1995 has yet to be beaten and is hailed as 'almost mythical' by doyens of the event. He holds the distinction of being a six-time world coal-carrying champion, yet that total has been surpassed by both Terry Lyons and John Hunter, who have each won the race on eight occasions. Lyons managed to win in eight years out of nine between 1977 and 1985. Janine Burns is the most successful-ever female coal carrier, lifting the title no fewer than eleven times. The women's record of four minutes twenty-five seconds was set by Batley's Catherine Fenton in 2011. In addition to the races for men and women, a veterans' race (for men over forty) was added in 2013 to mark the event's fiftieth year. Quite apart from the prestige of being able to claim world champion status, the prize money on offer is not to be sneezed at. The winner of the men's race receives £750 while the victorious woman gets £500, the figure jumping to £1,000 if either record is broken. That could buy you a lot of stove nuts.

Hundreds of spectators turn out to line the race route. 'It's a sheer blast of exertion,' says John Hunter – who has also won the Scottish Coal Carrying Championship – in an interview with BarBend. 'From the gun, you have to go flat out. People collapse, their legs go to jelly, they drop the bag and they just cannot pick it back up.' The sack is carried on the shoulders, and the grip is considered all-important to prevent it moving around too much or even falling. A handy tip is to grab hold of a solid lump of coal at the corners and hang on for dear life. The stamina-sapping course begins with a hill, but then flattens out before rising again. 'It plays tricks on your legs,' adds Hunter. 'It then flattens off again towards the end, so people sprint to the finish and their legs give way. I did it once and I was like Bambi, my legs just went out from under me.' Those three men in the pub have a lot to answer for.

The 2016 race was sponsored by a local funeral director. In view of the tremendous physical effort needed just to complete the course, perhaps he was hoping to drum up trade.

CHAPTER TWO

QUIRKY GAMES

BO-TAOSHI, JAPAN

Best described as a cross between rugby and war, the game of bo-taoshi ('knocking over pole') is an extreme version of Capture the Flag played by two teams of 150, each divided up into 75 attackers and 75 defenders. The game takes place on a rectangular field with two fifteen-foot-high wooden poles set some distance apart. Each pole is guarded by a human barrier of defenders. The object of the attackers is to capture the opponents' pole by lowering it to an angle of around thirty degrees from the ground before the other team's attackers succeed in doing the same to the other pole. Until a rule change in 1973, the angle needed to secure victory was only forty-five degrees. Someone somewhere obviously decided that bo-taoshi just wasn't brutal enough. That person probably works in corporate finance.

Although bo-taoshi looks like a free-for-all, there are apparently some rules to follow. While the defenders are limited to huddling around the pole, the attackers can move around the field at will. The defenders begin in a formation designed to guard the pole at all costs and wait for the inevitable onslaught. At the sound of a start gun, the attackers charge the defensive wall and simply trample over the human shield with no consideration for personal safety, their eyes fixed solely on the prize before them. Punching, kicking and gouging all appear perfectly permissible. The scene is not unlike the opening of the Boxing Day sales at Next. The pole must touch the ground at all times, and to try and ensure that it remains vertical a defending ninja sits at the top of the pole, using his weight to counteract the efforts of the attacking team. If the pole is being tilted, he must lean to the opposite side. He also acts as the last line of defence against any attacker who has managed to climb the pole, usually endeavouring to repel them with a swift kick to the face. The ninja therefore tends to be the team's most combative character, owing more to Charles Bronson than Charles Hawtrey. Other key positions in bo-taoshi are scrum (the attacking players who act as springboards for their team-mates to climb the pole and try to knock it down), pole attackers (who are in charge of toppling the ninja and using their weight to bring the pole down) and barrier (the bulk of the defenders who form a shield around the precious pole). All players don protective headgear but no footwear is worn in order to prevent attackers stomping on their opponents' faces while trying to climb the pole. A game can be over in just a couple of short but often painful minutes.

The game is believed to date back over seventy years and was supposedly invented as part of a training regime for the Japanese military. At its annual induction ceremony, the National Defence Academy of Japan organises a game between the new cadets. It is also played in many Japanese schools on sports days, even by nine- and ten-year-olds, although some academic institutions have banned it because of the high number of injuries. So if you think back to how much you complained about having to do cross-country at school, just be grateful that you weren't required to play bo-taoshi.

BOTTLE KICKING, HALLATON, LEICESTERSHIRE, ENGLAND

Bottle kicking in Hallaton is one of England's most physical sporting events. It dates back to 1771 and involves hundreds of players in two teams – one from Hallaton, the other from the neighbouring village of Medbourne – whose aim is to carry, kick or push two small wooden casks, known as 'bottles', over their goal line. It is essentially an excuse for a mass brawl among rival villagers, where anything goes apart from eye gouging, strangling and the use of weapons. It may therefore seem strange to first-time visitors to these shores that bottle kicking is filed away among 'quaint English customs' alongside gurning and morris dancing. Forget the morris men; this is GBH with bells on.

The contest takes place on Easter Monday, and is preceded by a ceremony known as the Hare Pie Scramble. This is said to date back to an occasion when two ladies from Hallaton, returning home across the fields, were confronted by a raging bull. As the beast bore down on them, a hare suddenly ran across its path, thus distracting it and allowing the ladies to escape. To show their gratitude, they instituted the custom of giving out hare pie once a year. The irony of rewarding something by slaughtering its relatives must have left the village blacksmith grateful that it was not he who had rescued the two damsels in distress. In addition to the hare pie, two barrels of beer were to be distributed to the village poor, but they fought among themselves for the food and drink, and on one occasion villagers from Medbourne joined the fray and snatched the beer. Incensed, the Hallatonians set aside their personal differences and joined forces to retrieve – by fair means or foul – what was rightfully theirs. Thus was born the rivalry between the two villages.

Following a parade and a church service at which the hare pie is blessed, the vicar throws pieces to the crowd for the scramble. Then it is time for the bottle kicking. Three small kegs are used in the contest. Two are filled with beer while the third, 'the dummy', is made of solid wood. Battle commences at the sign of each bottle being tossed in the air three times. The goals are two streams located a mile apart, and each team attempts to move the bottles across the stream by any means possible, although loading them into a vehicle or on horseback are prohibited. There is no limit to the number of participants, and in 2014 an estimated seven thousand people took part. The winning team is the first to force two bottles across the stream. To do so, players must overcome hedges, ditches and barbed wire as well as the opposing team. Injuries are routine and paramedics are usually on standby. At the end, the game's outstanding players – maybe someone who carried a bottle across the stream or managed to keep possession of it for some time – are helped to the top of the ten-foot-tall Buttercross landmark in Hallaton and the opened bottle is passed up for them to drink. The game, which resembles one gigantic, prolonged, ferocious rugby scrum, can last for several hours, even continuing after dark, by which time most of the participants are caked in mud, blood or both.

The rector of Hallaton tried to ban the event in 1790 but relented the next day after the words 'No pie, no parson' appeared scrawled on the vicarage walls. Since then it has taken place every year except 2001, when it was cancelled because of foot-and-mouth disease.

A similar ancient, rough-and-tumble tradition is the **Haxey Hood Game**, played in the Lincolnshire village of Haxey on the Twelfth Day of Christmas. Here, a mass scrum – or sway – forms to force a 'hood' (a three-foot-long leather tube) into a local pub, with each team battling to force it into their pub. As soon as the landlord can reach out and touch the 'hood', the game ends. It sounds simple, but because this is never done in a sensible, orderly fashion, the game invariably lasts for at least four hours.

BRAMBLE BANK CRICKET, THE SOLENT, HAMPSHIRE, ENGLAND

In normal cricket it is all too common for rain to stop play, but the annual Bramble Bank game must be the only one in the world where the tide stops play. That is because the pitch is a 200-yard-long sand bar in the middle of the Solent, the stretch of water between Hampshire and the Isle of Wight. The bar, known as Bramble Bank, only surfaces once a year (around the autumn equinox in September) for less than an hour before the waves wash in and swamp the pitch. But even though the outfield is, at its best, peppered with pools of water, that time is long enough for a yearly fixture between teams of cricket enthusiasts from the Royal Southern Yacht Club in Hamble on the mainland and the Island Sailing Club from Cowes – smack bang in the middle of one of the busiest shipping lanes in the world. To passengers on passing ships, it looks as though the players are walking on water.

The players sail out from the opposing coasts and wait eagerly in their boats for the moment when the bank becomes fit for play. Knowing that time is of the essence, they hurry to the field dressed in whites, trousers rolled up to the knee, and set up the stumps. Some prefer to play barefoot while others wear sandals. It is a pitch where gully is a natural formation rather than a fielding position, where the most distant fielding position is known as deep-water square leg, and where a duck can be a spectator as well as a score. Conditions can best be described as changeable, although the one thing that can be guaranteed is that there will be a little moisture in the wicket to encourage spin.

Bramble Bank was first used as a cricketing venue in the early twentieth century, but when yachtsman Uffa Fox organised a game there in 1954, it was the first such encounter since 1922.

Employing oars as bats, Fox's men scored 29, which was enough to defeat a team from Parkhurst Prison (principally officers) by seven runs. In fairness to Parkhurst, they were somewhat handicapped by the fact that only seven members of their team were able to land. Since the early 1970s, the game has become a regular fixture between the rival nautical clubs. It is very much a friendly fixture, with the result being decided beforehand as the two clubs take it in turns to win. It can draw as many as 150 spectators, all dotted around the bank in boats. At the 2012 game, some spectators had to be rescued by lifeboat after their boat's engine overheated.

Round-the-world sailor Sir Robin Knox-Johnston, who has represented the Royal Southern Yacht Club on a number of occasions, reveals the importance of tactical bowling when water is lapping around the ankles. He told *Yachts and Yachting*: 'The skill is to aim for the pool nearest the batsman and land the ball so it throws up a spray of sand into his face and stops dead so he can't hit it. Batting isn't easy. One year I was waved out: the ball landed in the water and a wave picked it up and hit my stumps, so I waded. I thought it was the gentlemanly thing to do.'

BRITISH AND WORLD MARBLES CHAMPIONSHIPS, TINSLEY GREEN, WEST SUSSEX, ENGLAND

Every Good Friday, hundreds of people gather in the car park of a pub in West Sussex to watch groups of otherwise sane adults lose their marbles. The Greyhound in Tinsley Green first staged the British and World Marbles Championships on Good Friday 1932, and it has remained the location ever since, described as a 'cathedral of marbles on an acre of asphalt in the shadow of Gatwick airport'. Sporting venues don't get any more romantic than that.

According to marbles folklore, the tournament actually dates back to 1588 during the reign of Elizabeth I when a young man from West Sussex and a young man from neighbouring Surrey were both vying for the hand of a Tinsley Green milk maiden. Unable to decide on a suitor, she set them a series of competitive tasks spanning an entire week (including such long-neglected pursuits as stoolball, tipcat and cock throwing), but after the twelve contests, the scores were tied at 6–6. Finally she told them to play marbles, because, with forty-nine marbles in the ring, there had to be an outright winner.

The rules have changed little since. A total of forty-nine red glass target marbles are placed in the centre of a raised sand-covered concrete ring that measures six foot in diameter. Two teams of six players take turns to try and hit the target marbles with their larger shooting marbles or 'tolleys'. The contest starts with a 'nose drop', where players drop their tolley from the tip of their nose to a line in the sand. The player whose tolley lands nearest to the line goes first. The shooting position is known as 'knuckling down' because the player forms a fist, knuckles pointing down, with the tolley resting on their thumbnail. A player's knuckle must rest on the ring. The aim is to knock as many of the target marbles out of the ring as possible, the first team to reach twenty-five winning the match. All the while, tournament officials keep a watchful eye for any 'fudging', the illegal forward movement of a player's hand during the act of shooting, or 'cabbaging', which is the term for deliberately shooting from the wrong spot.

The traditional British marbles playing season is Ash Wednesday to Good Friday – the period of Lent. Tournament organiser Sam McCarthy Fox, proud owner of around forty thousand marbles, explained to atlasobscura.com: 'Lent is a time where you have to give things up, and football and all the other sort of games were deemed to be too boisterous. But marbles was a nice little game that you could play during Lent.'

The event attracts around twenty teams each year. In the past, the international status was provided by entrants from France, Japan, Australia and the United States, but in recent years there has invariably been a strong German presence. In 2002, the Saxonia Globe Snippers became the first German team to win the tournament, and fellow countrymen 1st MC Erzgebirge went on to win on six occasions between 2006 and 2015. The most successful individual mibster (the technical term for a marbles player) is Len Smith who, in 1973, shot his way to a twelfth world title, and thus proved a worthy successor to legendary figures such as Jim 'Atomic Thumb' Longhurst, a wiry gardener with a powerful flick that could smash a beer glass from four feet, and Wee Willie Wright, a five-time winner of the individual title at Tinsley Green and renowned for his secret weapon, a hot water bottle sewn inside his coat to keep his thumb warm.

Marbles and controversy might seem unlikely bedfellows, but in 1970 there was uproar when the World Marbles Board of Control banned women from the championships because their mini-skirted bottoms were considered unsuitable and perhaps too distracting for the male players. A WMBC executive announced: 'Miniskirts are a disaster for marbles, and even in trousers or maxiskirts their bottoms are not suitable for the game. We couldn't limit the championships to women with size thirty-four hips or less, so we held a board meeting, studied photographs of the women in playing position and banned them altogether.' Mrs Irene Poole, captain of a rejected team from Brighton, was understandably aggrieved. 'It is nonsense to suggest that the sight of women crouching in miniskirts or trousers to flick marbles would put the men players off,' she said. 'Most women wear tights, so there would be no question of us revealing stocking tops and suspenders. In any case, the men should be concentrating on the game, not looking at our knees and bottoms!' The ban was subsequently lifted, and in 1987 an annual prize was introduced for the best female mibster. Today, many teams contain women players, and they can wear what they like.

The appeal of the event is summed up by John Roberts, a member of the Turners Hill Tolleymen, in an interview with vice. com: 'I founded the team back in 1981, and I've been coming here from when I was a kid. It's a social game. There's a lot of beer involved, and the spirit is to turn up and play. There are only a few games or sports where the taking part is the main thing.'

BUZKASHI, AFGHANISTAN

If you can imagine a game of polo where the ball is the headless gutted carcass of a dead goat, where riders wear tribal costume instead of neatly pressed shirts and white trousers, and where individual games used to last for several days, then you pretty much have buzkashi, the national sport of Afghanistan. In case you were left in any doubt as to the chief objective of the game, buzkashi translates as 'goat grabbing'. It is not a game for vegans.

Also known as kokpar (in Kazakhstan) and kokburu (in Kyrgyzstan), the game is thought to have first been played by the nomadic Turkic-Mongol peoples who spread westward from China and Mongolia around the thirteenth century. It is based on the practice of local tribesmen who used to steal goats or cattle while on horseback by scooping them up. Buzkashi is incredibly competitive – violence is not uncommon – and matches in Afghanistan, where the best riders acquire hero status, draw thousands of fans. Although traditionally games used to go on for days, to make the sport more spectator-friendly a time limit of two forty-five-minute halves has been introduced. Interestingly, the game was banned in Afghanistan during the Taliban regime because they considered it immoral. To be considered too extreme for the Taliban gives a fair indication of exactly how wild buzkashi can be.

Described by *Time* magazine as 'Afghanistan's favourite form of organised mayhem', buzkashi involves two or more teams of ten riders on horseback battling for control of the goat carcass. In some games, only five riders from each team are allowed on the field at the same time. The day before the game, the goat is slaughtered, beheaded, disembowelled and relieved of its legs. It is then soaked in water for twenty-four hours to toughen it and prevent it being shredded in the ensuing tussle. Occasionally sand is packed into the carcass to give it extra weight. In the absence of a suitable goat, other slaughtered animals are also available for play, such as calves or sheep. In fact, top-level games often use calves because their carcasses are heavier. A goal is scored by wrestling the carcass from the opposing team, carrying it around a flag at one end of the 400-metre-square playing field and then dropping it in a chalk circle at the opposite end. Participants carry short whips, with which they are allowed to hit opponents' horses but not – at least according to the rules – the opposition riders. However, elbowing, punching, kicking and other forms of close physical combat are positively encouraged, although biting, hair pulling and deliberately knocking an opponent off his horse are liable to incur the wrath of the referee. If the field is located near a river, drowning an opponent is also considered unsportsmanlike.

When not in use, the whip is typically carried between the teeth, leaving the riders' hands free for horse steering and carcass grabbing. While escaping with the carcass, the rider usually tucks it under his leg. To protect themselves from other players' whips and boots, the riders wear heavy clothing. In some countries, they go a step further by wearing salvaged Soviet tank helmets. The boots have high heels that lock into the horse's saddle so that the rider can lean on the side of the horse while trying to pick up the goat. Some ram wooden or metal rods down the boots for extra protection, as a collision with a horse can easily result in a broken leg. The winning team is usually the one that best combines horsemanship, strength and courage – three highly prized commodities in Afghan culture – and to become a champion buzkashi rider, or *chapandaz*, is the stuff of dreams for many an Afghan boy. It is one that most men do not achieve until they are in their forties. To be a *chapandaz* in Afghanistan is a great honour; to be a goat is not such good news.

CALCIO STORICO, FLORENCE, ITALY

Calcio storico is an early form of football that originated in sixteenth-century Italy, where its popularity was such that popes often played it. No doubt there was a queue outside the confessional box the next day of victorious players seeking divine forgiveness for defeating the Vatican team. The game was largely reserved for wealthy aristocrats but it gradually fell out of favour before being revived by Mussolini in 1930. Today, three matches are played annually in the third week of June in Florence's Piazza Santa Croce. The teams represent the four quarters of the city – Santa Croce (the blues), Santa Maria Novella (the reds), Santo Spirito (the whites), and San Giovanni (the greens). After two semi-finals, the winners go on to meet in the grand final on 24 June, which is the Day of San Giovanni, the Patron Saint of Florence. Given the highly physical nature of the game, the Patron Saint of Head-Butting might be a more appropriate choice.

For this is not football as we know it. Two teams of twenty-seven a side fight it out on a pitch covered in sand sixteen inches deep. The players start wearing medieval costume but usually end up bare-chested. The pitch is about eighty metres long and forty metres wide, and a four-foot-high goal net runs along the width of each end. To score a goal (or *caccia*), a player must kick or throw the ball into the opposing net. If he sends the ball above the net, his team is awarded only half a *caccia*. The scoring of each goal is marked by the firing of a small cannon.

Each team is made up of four goalkeepers, three fullbacks, five halfbacks and fifteen forwards. The game begins with a match official directing the ball towards the centre line, whereupon the opposing forwards proceed to beat the hell out of one another, supposedly in an attempt to gain possession of the ball, although at times the settling of personal vendettas appears to make the presence of the ball purely incidental. Head-butting, choking, punching, elbowing, wrestling, kicking and martial arts techniques are all deemed perfectly legitimate tactics. Only kicking in the head and blindside punching are barred, and it is also illegal for more than one player to attack an opponent simultaneously. Any violation results in the offending player being thrown out of the game. Once enough opposing forwards are incapacitated (there are no substitutions for injuries), team-mates try and force the ball into the goal.

Matches last fifty minutes and frequently descend into wholesale wanton violence. Ears have been lost in the middle of a scrum, and players have ended up in comas following illegal punches to the back of the head. One player who had his shaved scalp sliced open by an opponent says: 'When you're playing, you don't feel any of it. But then you calm down and take a shower. And that is when everything starts to burn.' After a particularly brutal final in 2013, ten players required hospital treatment. On average, it is estimated that as many as eight players from each team are unable to finish the game due to injury. The referee and six linesmen desperately try to act as peacekeepers, but this is no easy task when the average calcio storico player makes Vinnie Jones look like Mother Teresa.

In medieval times, the winning team were presented with a cow; now they receive a free dinner. It all seems a lot of effort for a couple of slices of pizza.

CHESSBOXING, LONDON, ENGLAND

If asked to invent a hybrid sport, most of us would probably come up with something like a mixture of skiing and diving (skiving). But Dutch performance artist Iepe Rubingh possessed a more active imagination and saw the potential for combining the passive aggression of chess with the aggressive passion of boxing. So he came up with the sport of chessboxing, where competitors fight in alternating rounds of chess and boxing, the ultimate test of brain and brawn.

Some historians of the discipline claim that it dates back to 1970s London when young brothers James and Stuart Robinson developed a routine of fighting at their boxing club in Kidbrooke before sitting down to play each other at chess. This practice continued for three years, but it failed to catch on with their fellow boxing club members, who branded them 'idiots'. However, Rubingh was inspired by a 1992 French comic book by Enki Bilal, which showed a chessboxing world championship where, like the Robinsons, opponents fought each other for an entire boxing match and then played each other at chess. Rubingh decided this was impractical, and instead elected to alternate rounds of chess and boxing, which, to outsiders, sounded even more impractical.

Undeterred, he developed a definitive set of rules for the new sport. A chessboxing contest lasts eleven three-minute rounds – six of chess and five of boxing, beginning and ending with a round of chess. The break between each round is one minute, during which boxers are strongly advised to remove their gloves before attempting to move their chess pieces. As in standard boxing bouts, there are distinct weight classes, so that a puny nerd does not have to step into the ring with a hulking brute. Victory can be obtained by checkmate or a player exceeding the time limit (chess), knockout or technical knockout (boxing) and disqualifica-tion or resignation (both). If a player knocks out his opponent at chess, he will almost certainly be disqualified. In the event of no outright victory at either discipline, the one who is ahead on boxing points is declared the winning chessboxer. The hardest part is said to be adjusting to the calm mindset of chess after three minutes of fighting. Occasionally the aggression from the boxing ring can spill over on to the chessboard, but happily there have been few recorded instances of a player bashing his bishop in public.

The first official chessboxing contest took place in Berlin in 2003, and later that year the first world championship fight was held in Amsterdam between Rubingh and his fellow Dutch middleweight Jean Louis Veenstra. Fittingly, Rubingh won in the eleventh and final round after his opponent exceeded the chess time limit. My sport, my title.

The novelty value particularly appealed to the German public and by 2006, crowds of 800 were commonplace for chessboxing contests. The sport rapidly spread to the UK, USA, India and Russia, and in 2011 the unthinkable happened when chessboxing turned professional. In 2015, fifty-seven-year-old former IBF light welterweight world champion Terry Marsh returned to the ring after an absence of nearly thirty years for the GrandMaster BASH! chessboxing match in London. 'I have always played chess and I have always boxed,' he told the *Evening Standard*. 'To be perfectly honest. I'm expecting to get bashed up and will be relying on the chess to pull me through it.' His opponent, Armenia's Dymer Agasaryan, was thirty-four years his junior and the reigning World Chessboxing Association middleweight champion. After a shaky start, Marsh found his feet in the ring, captured a dangerous pawn and went on to take the world title. The event was put on by

London Chessboxing, who now regularly stage contests in the capital. Chessboxing looks like it is here to stay, meaning that sports promoters are constantly looking for the next big thing. Anyone for Sumo Scrabble?

COW-PAT BINGO, TROMSØ, NORWAY

If you want to combine a game of bingo with the great outdoors, try your hand at cow-pat bingo. It may not promise fresh air – indeed, the air around the bingo field is anything but fresh – but it contains all the drama of the indoor version with a pungent, bovine twist. And it can last ten times as long. The premise is simple: a fenced-in field is marked out into a grid of squares, each measuring about three foot. Each square is numbered, and punters gamble on which square the cow will deposit its first poop when it is released into the enclosure. In the event of the animal dropping its load on more than one square, that with the biggest volume of excrement is declared the winner. In particularly close contests, this may need to be decided with the aid of rubber gloves, a set of scales and a strong nose. In local variations, some games determine the winner by whatever square the right front leg of the cow is in at the time of the drop. Other games may provide more than one winner by waiting for the cow to do a second poop or by introducing a second cow.

The game has been around for some years, primarily in North America, where it is called cow-patty bingo and is popular at state fairs. However, it recently made a big splat in Norway, where under the name of *kuskit bingo*, it formed part of Langfjorddagan 2015, a festival in the north of the country. Preparation consists of little more than feeding the animals well beforehand to guarantee that there is a winner, but even so, it took fifty minutes and a number of false alarms before the Norwegian cow finally dumped on H6, winning one lucky onlooker a new camera. In a country that has pioneered the concept of Slow TV, where prime-time television has been known to consist of eight hours of knitting or twelve hours watching a log fire burn, nobody seemed worried that the game took the best part of an hour. 'It was exciting,' said one punter. 'A wonderful and creative idea of slow bingo.'

In 2002, the game was at the centre of an unprecedented furore when organisers of a contest in Lakeland, Florida were accused of feeding the cows laxatives beforehand to ensure a swift result. The organisers denied the allegations. Occasionally a time limit of an hour is set for the cow to do its business, and if nothing has happened by then, it is declared a stalemate. This is because, after sixty minutes spent in close proximity to a cow's backside, spectators are inclined to remark to one another: 'Blimey, it smells a bit stale, mate.'

ELFEGO BACA SHOOTOUT GOLF TOURNAMENT,
SOCORRO, NEW MEXICO, USA

The Elfego Baca Shootout is the epitome of crazy golf – a one-hole, one-day shootout from a tee positioned on the summit of Socorro Peak in New Mexico to a 'green' 2,550 feet below and nearly three miles away. To reach the actual hole – a fifty-foot circle chalked in the desert dirt – golfers must whack and hack their way down the mountain's rocky terrain and encounter such hazards as 100-foot canyons, mineshafts, rattlesnakes, scorpions and the occasional mountain lion. Never again will a tricky lie on a slight downslope or a second shot that requires lofting the ball over a small bush seem such a big deal.

The shootout – named after Wild West sheriff Elfego Baca – was devised in 1960 to drum up publicity for the quiet college town of Socorro and is now a side event on the final day of the Socorro Open tournament. The player who records the lowest score on the marathon hole is named that year's shootout champion. The course record is nine strokes, which is mightily impressive considering that the average club golfer would probably be lucky to break fifty. Ominously the scorecard goes up to seventy-five. For this isn't a course where you only lose balls; out there you could lose three-quarters of a foursome.

After scaling the summit of the mountain in four-by-four vehicles, the golfers tee off from a wooden platform and begin the long scramble down. Lugging a full bag of clubs is not an option, so most take just a driver and something like a five-iron . . . along with a first-aid kit, binoculars, bug spray, and a pair of tweezers for pulling cactus needles out of flesh. As the boulder-strewn landscape is as far removed from the neatly cut fairways of Augusta as imaginable and any grass takes the form of menacing tufts sprouting out of rock crevices, players are allowed to tee up the ball for every shot. For this purpose, many golfers carry around a square of old carpet, an empty water bottle or even a small broom that can be jammed handle-down into the ground. Since every lie would be declared unplayable on a normal golf course, players are permitted to move their ball up to a distance of fifty feet, provided that doing so does not leave it closer to the hole. Each golfer is allowed ten balls and must finish with at least one. Any ball that can't be found within twenty minutes counts as an extra stroke. This is a frequently incurred penalty because if the ball has rolled down into a canyon, it could take closer to twenty days to find it. Three spotters, whose job it is to locate the ball, are allocated to each competitor. Their role is crucial.

Eighteen-time Elfego Baca champion Mike Stanley (average score eighteen) told ESPN: 'You've got to hit the ball where they can find it. You try to hit it right to the top of a cliff if you can, so you're strategically positioned for the next shot. Although the elevation drop can help you smash drives great distances, a lot of times it's not how far you hit it but where. The hardest thing to do is get a stance built so you can stand and swing and not fall down. You pile up rocks, you dig with your feet, anything.'

Even when golfers are in sight of the target 'green', there is work to be done as it is extremely challenging to stop the ball within the circle on such hard, barren land. Players often take up to seven hours to complete the hole, and in summer, when temperatures can top 100 degrees, just reaching the bottom of the mountain without needing assistance from the emergency medical team is considered an achievement. Fittingly, in Spanish 'socorro' means 'help'.

So why bother? 'It's a once-in-a-lifetime thing to go to the top of a mountain and play your way down,' says local golf professional Miguel Griego. 'You're never going to get another chance to hit your first shot 1,000 yards.'

FOOTBALL IN THE RIVER, BOURTON-ON-THE-WATER, GLOUCESTERSHIRE, ENGLAND

The only thing you can guarantee about the annual football match held in the Cotswolds on August Bank Holiday Monday is that the pitch will be waterlogged. For it takes place in the shallow waters of the usually tranquil River Windrush in picturesque Bourton-on-the Water. Two teams of six from local club Bourton Rovers play with a conventional football but while standing in water that reaches just above their ankles. The goalposts are set up in front of the two main bridges in the centre of the village, making the pitch around fifty yards long and nine yards wide. With so much water about, the most popular cry from the sidelines is 'bring on the sub!'

The game has been played for more than a hundred years and draws large crowds lining the riverbank. Spectators are strongly advised to wear waterproof clothing even on a sunny day because excessive splashing is one of the game's trademarks. Players wear footwear to protect their feet from the stony river bed and the only time they step on to dry land is to take throw-ins. Long throws are a feature of the game as they are one way of ensuring that the ball remains airborne and therefore travels quickly from one end of the pitch to the other, turning defence into attack. This is essential because progress through the water is severely restricted. David Beckham may have been routinely able to strike shots from thirty yards on grass, but in the hurly-burly of the River Windrush he would struggle to manage thirty inches. The key to success is to flick the ball up out of the water and then volley it towards goal. A referee is on hand to keep some semblance of order and to see that the rules of Association Football are generally adhered to, while making allowances for the setting.

Foul tackles are virtually impossible to detect amid the splashing, although deliberately pushing over an opponent and then holding him underwater may be considered an infringement. The match lasts around fifteen minutes each half, depending on the temperature of the water. This rarely rises much above cold.

Although the origins of the game are unclear, match organiser Matt Winter told lovingthecotswolds.com: 'Rumour has it that it was started by some men who were bored, so to break the boredom they decided to jump into the river and have a kickabout, and it's carried on ever since. The teams that play are Bourton first team against Bourton reserves, so there's a bit at stake in the bragging rights. Although it only lasts about half an hour, it's hard work – you ache for days and days after.'

One thing the players definitely don't need at the final whistle is a bath.

IRISH ROAD BOWLING, COUNTY
ARMAGH, NORTHERN IRELAND

Instead of playing on beautifully manicured greens, the sport of road bowling – or bullets – takes place on twisty, tarmac country lanes with players propelling a metal ball along a predetermined course of around two miles in as few throws as possible. This is cross-country bowls. The game has been around since the seventeenth century, but is now largely confined to Ireland (especially County Armagh in the north and Cork in the south) and Irish communities in North America. In fact, the largest Irish road bowling event in the world takes place not in Ireland but in Wheeling, West Virginia, where 737 bowlers convened for a tournament in September 2016. It's not quite up with Guinness in the export stakes but it's getting there.

The bowl or 'bullet' is an iron and steel cannonball three inches in diameter and weighing 28 ounces. Games can be played individually or as teams. Under the old rules, players were given twenty shots (a score) to see who could cover the greatest total distance with their bowls, but now the winner is the one who reaches the finish line in the fewest shots. If two players approach the finish line in the same number of shots, the victor is decided by whose throw goes further past. Throws of half a mile are not uncommon in road bowling, particularly on downhill sections of road. Understandably, long uphill stretches tend to be avoided altogether. Playing road bowls up a steep mountain pass would be a thankless task, liable to go on for days.

Each thrower is assisted by a road shower who, rather like a caddy in golf, offers advice about the shot. Another helper stands ahead of the thrower, feet apart in the manner of a croquet hoop, to illustrate the best line to take in order to avoid prematurely ending up in a ditch or in someone's front garden. The thrower then runs up to the throwing mark – or 'butt' – and releases the bowl underhand before stepping over the mark. Ideally, the bowl should fly through the air for a few yards before landing and rolling. As a guide to the thrower, team-mates will often place a tuft of grass – or 'sop' – in the road at the spot where they want the bowl to hit the road surface. Leading throwers cunningly apply topspin to gain extra distance, this tactic often proving more effective and accurate than an almighty hurl. Wherever the bowl eventually comes to rest, a chalk mark is made at the nearest point on the road and the next throw is taken from behind that mark. Where there is a tight corner or a junction, the player may take the aerial route by lofting the bowl, but it must still land on or pass over the road. If the loft falls short of the road, it counts as a penalty shot, with the next throw being taken from the same mark. In road bowling terminology, a 'butt breaker' is a player who has accidentally stepped over the mark before releasing the bowl, rather than someone with excessive flatulence. Presumably, therefore, 'butt craic' describes the banter involving a player who has overstepped the mark.

The sport attracts a considerable amount of betting, and, as such has not been without controversy. At one point, the Cork authorities tried to have the game outlawed, and right up until the 1950s road bowlers were being fined and even threatened with jail. However, when the first All-Ireland Championships between Armagh and Cork were held in 1963, over 20,000 spectators turned up in Armagh to see local man Danny McPartland beat Cork's Derry Kenny over a three-mile course on the final shot by just eleven yards. Sadly a few years later, the roads of County Armagh would ring to the sound of a more sinister kind of bullet.

KABADDI, BANGLADESH

The simple game of tag or 'it' has long been a familiar playground pastime in British schools. You would ruthlessly hunt down a child, touch them and declare that he or she was 'it' and had the dreaded lurgy. The temptation was always to seek out the slowest, bulkiest child because they were less likely to outpace you and also offered the biggest target area. If the poor wretch was tagged just before the end of break, they faced the prospect of having to remain 'it' all the way through the next lesson, which could be a traumatic experience. Even the teacher somehow seemed to sense that a pupil was 'it' by asking a devilish question that proved a struggle to answer. Which is hardly surprising because it's very difficult to concentrate on your nine times table when you've been told you've got the lurgy, a disease so contagious that it could be passed on just by touching. All things considered, it's a miracle any child victim emerged from a game of tag without being emotionally scarred for life.

Tag is also the basis for kabaddi – the national sport of Bangladesh – but with the added proviso that players must hold their breath while tagging opponents. Consequently, purple faces and bulging eyes are not uncommon on the kabaddi field. The school nurse would definitely not have approved.

In standard kabaddi, two teams of seven occupy opposite halves of the field and take turns to send a 'raider' into the opposing half. The whole time the raider is in the opposing half he must hold his breath and continuously shout 'kabaddi, kabaddi, kabaddi' with his exhaling breath to show the referee that he has not inhaled. If he stops chanting 'kabaddi, kabaddi, kabaddi' for any reason – even if he has merely forgotten the words – he is considered 'out'. The raider's aim is to tag an opponent using either hand or leg before returning to his own half. Each opponent he tags earns his team a point. If, however, the raider is tackled, wrestled to the ground and prevented from returning before he needs to inhale, the opponents win the point. Tagged members who do not manage to catch the raider who tagged them are declared to be 'out' and are temporarily sent from the field. If an entire opposing team is declared 'out' at any one time, a bonus of two points is awarded. This is called a lona. The attributes of a good kabaddi player therefore are speed, strength and, above all, a decent set of lungs.

The sport, which is played by men and women and has recently caught on in Britain, originated in India some 4,000 years ago but did not receive international exposure until India demonstrated it at the 1936 Olympics in Berlin. The most popular version is played with two twenty-minute halves. Since 2004, there has been a Kabaddi World Cup tournament, in which India has reigned supreme, although sadly the rules for that have been changed so that tagging raiders now have thirty seconds to return to their half and no longer need to hold their breath and repeat 'kabaddi, kabaddi, kabaddi'. To the impartial observer, this seems to have taken away the very essence of the game, like removing the net in tennis. Progress is not always for the better.

LINGERIE FOOTBALL, USA

Perhaps it was the success of beach volleyball that made promoters believe that men would happily pay good money to watch women play sports while wearing skimpy clothing. The idea of women playing American football in little more than bra and panties may have been lurking darkly in what passes for a television executive's mind for decades, but it was at the 2004 Super Bowl that it first became reality when, as an alternative to the usual half-time entertainment, a TV special called the Lingerie Bowl was aired opposite it as a pay-per-view event. The concept attracted enough subscribers to be repeated for the next two Super Bowls, and in 2009, one Mitch Mortaza, a former contestant on *Blind Date*, decided to expand it from a single exhibition game to form the ten-team Lingerie Football League. Team names such as the Dallas Desire, the Los Angeles Temptation, the Philadelphia Passion, the Las Vegas Sin, the Chicago Bliss, the San Diego Seduction and the Orlando Fantasy give some indication of its target audience. No sign then of the Houston Headaches, the Tallahassee Too Tireds or the Nashville Not in the Moods.

Although, as expected, it attracted plenty of media attention, the Lingerie Football League wanted to be taken seriously for making a bona fide contribution to women's sport. So, in 2013, it changed its name to the Legends Football League and switched its tagline from 'True Fantasy Football' to 'Women of the Gridiron'. More importantly, the trademark garters, bras and panties were tossed in the sin bin, replaced by marginally less scanty 'performance apparel'. Although the new outfits were meant to owe more to Adidas than Ann Summers, from a distance only a seasoned voyeur would have been able to spot the difference. Even so, those who accused the players of dressing for the bedroom were wide of the mark, unless the woman in their life happens to wear a helmet and shoulder pads in bed. 'Just because we play in the LFL does not mean we promote promiscuity,' said Abbie Sullivan of the Cleveland Crush to cantonrep. com. 'We are smart females. We are athletes who take care of our bodies. We are the total package. It's about football and we're actually pretty good at it.' Although the players also wear knee and elbow pads, many thought that the amount of flesh still on display left them more susceptible to injury than was necessary. It was felt in some quarters that safety could be improved if the players' uniforms were designed more for protection and less for titillation.

The seven-a-side league operates under the same principles as the men's game except there are no field goals and no punts. By the end of 2013, lingerie – sorry, legends, football – had been adopted in Australia and Canada. Take a bow, the Saskatoon Sirens.

In 2015, the success of the American model inspired twenty-three-year-old Manchester-based Gemma Hughes to found Lingerie Football League UK with the aim of creating a soccer tournament in which the players wore crop tops and short shorts. Her aim was to attract much-needed sponsorship to the women's game. She told the *Daily Mirror*: 'We know this is scandalous, we know it's controversial, but that media attention is what's going to sell tickets. This is not about the players looking beautiful or sexy. We want to break the stigma that [women's] football is just for tomboys.' However, it all kicked off in the press amid accusations of sexism and the Football Association dismissed the idea of lingerie football as a publicity stunt. Although the players have taken part in occasional charity matches in the north-west, it seems it might be a while before they get to run out at Old Trafford or Anfield. In the meantime, men wishing to ogle leggy blondes playing football will have to make do with Peter Crouch.

MUGGLE QUIDDITCH, MIDDLEBURY, VERMONT, USA

Quidditch is one of those rare sports that is based on a fictional game – namely that devised by author J.K. Rowling in her Harry Potter books. It has become more popularly known as muggle quidditch to distinguish it from Rowling's version, which involves flying broomsticks and enchanted balls. In the world of Harry Potter, a 'muggle' is a person incapable of performing magic, and although players in the real game do have a broomstick between their legs, they definitely cannot fly – even after a rousing pre-match team talk from the coach.

Muggle quidditch is played by two teams of seven (no more than four of the same gender) mounted on broomsticks. Each team is composed of three chasers, two beaters, one keeper and one seeker. The rectangular pitch has three hoops of varying heights at either end. The rules are simple. To score ten points, chasers or keepers must get the quaffle (a slightly deflated volleyball) into one of the three opposing hoops. To prevent the quaffle from advancing down the pitch, chasers and keepers are able to tackle their opposing numbers at the same time as beaters use one of the three bludgers (a dodgeball) to take out opponents. Once a player is hit by an opposing bludger, that player must dismount their broom, drop any ball being held, and touch their hoops before being allowed back into play. After seventeen minutes of this, the snitch (a tennis ball in a long yellow sock attached to the back of the snitch runner's shorts) is released on to the pitch, followed a minute later by the two opposing seekers. The game ends when the snitch is caught by one of the seekers, awarding thirty points for that team. The winning team is the one with most points accumulated. And you thought the offside rule in football was complicated.

The sport was created in 2005 at Middlebury College, Vermont by students Xander Manshel and Alex Benepe, who drew up the first of many rulebooks. At that first game, players wore capes fashioned from towels and one, unable to locate a broomstick, rode a standard lamp instead. It flourished so rapidly that by 2007 there was an International Quidditch Association World Cup, which was won by Middlebury. The 2016 tournament in Frankfurt, Germany was won by Australia, handing the United States their first ever loss in a grand final. Although the game is still played at Middlebury, it has become an international sport, with teams in more than twenty-five countries, from Argentina to Australia, Belgium to Brazil, and Canada to China. It is estimated that around twenty thousand people play the game worldwide. There is also an annual European Quidditch Cup, and in 2017, the Quidditch Premier League was formed in the UK, split into two geographical sections, each containing four teams. People may scoff, but at the rate the BBC is haemorrhaging sports events, Gary Lineker may soon find himself presenting muggle quidditch highlights on a Saturday night … provided the live wife carrying from Dorking doesn't overrun.

ROBOT SOCCER WORLD CUP

'By the middle of the twenty-first century, a team of fully autonomous humanoid robot soccer players shall win a soccer game, complying with the official rules of FIFA, against the winner of the most recent World Cup.' That was the ambitious goal behind the Robot Soccer World Cup – or RoboCup – an international robotics competition launched in 1997.

RoboCup has gone on to become an annual event. The first contest, in Nagoya, Japan, to where it returned in 2017, attracted thirty-eight teams from eleven countries. By the 2010 event in Singapore, there were 500 teams from 40 countries.

Machines dribble, tackle and shoot in a range of different categories, including those for humanoids of all sizes (these have two arms and two legs), non-humanoids and four-legged robots. If you have ever wondered what a game of football would be like played between two teams of dogs, the four-legged RoboCup provides the answer. It is not entirely lifelike, however, because the first thing any small dog is likely to do at kick-off is pee on the ball.

Once the game is underway, the robots have to fend for themselves. Humans are not allowed to amend the programming. Sean Harris, a member of the New South Wales University team that won the 58-centimetre-tall humanoid section for Australia in 2015, explained to the *International Business Times*: 'They tell everyone else where they are on the field and where the ball is. And they make decisions. Maybe one player will play goalkeeper and another says I'm closest to the ball, I'm going to kick it. They try and position around the field and they share all that information. Everyone has the same robots, so it's all about how you programme them and the intelligence. But we have a really fast walk, so we get to the ball first. And we can play in the direction we want to. That wins us most of the games.' At that year's competition the traditional red ball was replaced by a white ball, which was harder for the robots to spot. As a result, there was an increasing tendency for the players to kick each other, mistaking them for the ball. 'The kicking is most likely unintentional,' Professor Daniel Polani, manager of England's representatives from the University of Hertfordshire, told BBC News. 'We don't yet have robots that understand that kicking will hurt other robots.' The new Astroturf-like playing surface also meant that the players struggled to stay upright, often falling over after kicking the ball. Just as kicking an opponent is not considered a foul in robot football, the players are no doubt relieved that the referees take a lenient view on simulation.

In 2016, automated referee software was used to control some of the matches for the first time. So not all of the referees were human, thus bringing RoboCup in line with the Premier League.

As for defeating human World Cup winners by 2050, the experts point to the huge strides that have been made by robot footballers in recent years and suggest that the possibility is 'not entirely unrealistic'. That's a 'no' then.

SHROVETIDE FOOTBALL, ASHBOURNE, DERBYSHIRE, ENGLAND

Any similarity between Shrovetide football, one of England's oldest sports events, and Association Football is purely coincidental. Like bottle kicking, it is basically a mass brawl in which the ball often disappears for hours at a time, meaning that the chances of winning a Shrovetide football Spot-the-Ball competition are slimmer than those of collecting the EuroMillions jackpot.

Shrovetide football dates back hundreds of years, one theory being that the 'ball' was originally a severed head tossed into the crowd following an execution. Sedgefield in County Durham claims to have played it in 1027, but the earliest written record belongs to Chester in 1533. Being a Puritan, Philip Stubbes was naturally not a fan of anything that passed as entertainment. In his 1583 diatribe *The Anatomie of Abuses*, he wrote: 'For as concerning football playing, I protest unto you that it may rather be called a friendly kind of fight than a play or recreation ... And hereof groweth envy, malice, rancour, choler, hatred, displeasure, enmity, and what not else; and sometimes fighting, brawling, contention, quarrel picking, murder, and great effusion of blood.' It is safe to say that Mrs Stubbes – if such a woman existed – would not have needed to hunt out Phil's rosette and rattle on a Saturday afternoon.

The most famous Shrovetide football game, first recorded in 1682, takes place at Ashbourne in Derbyshire between the Up'ards (those born north of the River Henmore) and the Down'ards (those born to the south). The two goals are the millstones at the now demolished mills of Clifton (where the Down'ards score) and Sturston (where the Up'ards score). These are located three miles apart, making this a seriously big pitch. For a goal to be scored, the ball has to be struck against the millstone three successive times. Contrary to the rules of modern football, the teams attempt to carry the ball back towards their own goal rather than their opponents'. The leather ball, which is slightly larger than a conventional football, is painted for the occasion and filled with cork, partly to discourage long kicking but also to help it float when it inevitably ends up in the shallow Henmore that runs between the two goals. Indeed, the position of the millstones means that the scorer must actually be in the water to score a goal. The ball may be carried, thrown or kicked, but usually makes painfully slow progress in a series of rugby-like 'hugs', made up of hundreds of people. During these 'hugs', the ball is usually invisible to spectators. The ball may not be carried in a motorised vehicle or secreted in a bag or rucksack, and cemeteries, churchyards and the town's Memorial Gardens are strictly out of bounds. Players are also told not to climb over parked cars.

The game is played over two days on Shrove Tuesday and Ash Wednesday, starting at 2 p.m. each day with the ball being 'turned up' (thrown to the players) and continuing until well into the night at 10 p.m. If a goal is scored before 6 p.m., a new ball is released and play restarts from the town centre; otherwise play ends for the day. The goal scorers are chosen in advance, so when the ball reaches the goal, it is handed to the member of that team who has been awarded the honour of actually goaling the ball. This is almost always the member of a local family, meaning that it is nigh on impossible for a visitor or a tourist to score a goal. Afterwards, the scorer is carried on the shoulders of his teammates into the courtyard of the Green Man Hotel.

The raucous nature of Shrovetide football has frequently upset the authorities, and in 1891 the police made a determined effort to prevent the Ashbourne game taking place, only for the ball to be smuggled in under a lady's skirt. By 1928, however, it had acquired such respectability that the then Prince of Wales (later Edward VIII) was invited to Ashbourne to start the game. He even took part and, although he ended up with a bloody nose for his trouble, his involvement allowed the game to claim royal status, a fact confirmed in 2003 when Prince Charles 'turned up' the ball but wisely refrained from joining the 'hug'. The game continued to be played annually throughout both World Wars (indeed, the Ashbourne Regiment played a version in the German trenches during the First World War), but foot-and-mouth disease caused its cancellation in 1968 and 2001. In 1966, huge crowds showed up to watch former England footballer Stanley Matthews start proceedings.

For obvious reasons, spectators are urged to park their cars well away from the main streets, and the shops in the town centre are boarded up for the duration of the game lest any stray shopper should suddenly experience the sensation of being trampled underfoot by a herd of marauding wildebeest while he or she is on her way to Sainsbury's.

SLAMBALL, LOS ANGELES, USA

How many of us have watched a game of basketball and thought: 'You know what the problem with this sport is? The players just aren't tall enough. Wouldn't it be better if they were ten, twelve or even fifteen feet tall?' In the absence of a superhero breeding programme, an American sports enthusiast by the name of Mason Gordon came up with the concept of SlamBall. It is essentially a high-octane version of basketball played on trampolines, allowing players to launch themselves into orbit to land baskets. However, whereas physical contact is strictly limited in basketball, SlamBall players can prevent a score by deliberately smashing into each other in mid-air, like a crazy video game. This is sport as played by Crash Bandicoot.

A SlamBall court has four trampolines in front of each net with four players from each team on the court at any one time. There are three positions – handler (the dribbler), gunner (the shooter) and stopper (the defender). Teams can choose their own configuration but often start with two handlers. A turnover of possession occurs if two players from the same team find themselves on the same trampoline and if an attacking player bounces twice on a trampoline while in possession of the ball. Other rules are vaguely similar to basketball except that players wear helmets and padding to protect themselves from injury. Apparently its major appeal is that it gives players who are under six foot tall the opportunity to slam-dunk. 'When you come off those trampolines you feel like you are floating,' said one. 'For little people to be above the rim is a new feeling. You can't have fear playing this sport. There is no other sport where you have physical contact fourteen feet in the air.' Except perhaps paragliding for beginners.

The new sport started out in a small warehouse in Los Angeles around 2001 on a makeshift court cobbled together from spare parts, but within a year 400 people had been enlisted as potential players. In 2002, SlamBall made its debut on US TV and a six-team American league was formed but that dissolved after two seasons before briefly resurfacing five years later. The old TV shows have since been screened in Italy, China and Australia, leading to the establishment of SlamBall Asia and a World Championship Series. Gordon still harbours dreams of one day seeing SlamBall as an Olympic sport, and who knows, the introduction of trampolines could provide a much-needed stimulus to other Olympic disciplines. It would certainly create a new challenge for the archers and would see the triple jump record come on in leaps and bounds.

TUK TUK POLO TOURNAMENT, GALLE, SRI LANKA

Until 2007, an elephant polo tournament in the southern port city of Galle was among Sri Lanka's major sporting attractions, drawing tourists from far and wide. But that year one of the elephants went on the rampage and smashed several spectators' cars, causing the event to be cancelled on the grounds of animal cruelty. The missing elephants left a large hole in the Galle sporting calendar, but in 2015 ex-pat Australian hotelier Geoffrey Dobbs had the bright idea of replacing them with motorised tuk tuks (or auto rickshaws), the little open-sided, three-wheeled vehicles that trundle around as taxis in many areas of Asia. So was born the Tuk Tuk Polo Championships, staged first on a friendly basis but by February 2016 as a proper eight-team tournament with a first prize of $1,430. The spectacle of these milk floats with attitude battling it out proved so popular that it has become an annual event.

There are three tuk tuks in each team, and each vehicle contains two people – a driver and a player. The driver, as you might expect, sits in the driver's seat and steers the thing while the player sits in the back seat and leans out to strike the ball with a mallet, often just inches away from an opponent's wheels. The player has to direct the driver (like a tuk tuk TomTom) who in turn has to avoid wrapping his fragile vehicle around an opponent. The aim, as with normal horseback polo, is to score goals by hitting the ball between the opposing team's goalposts located at either end of the field. Ball control is not easy on the hard, bumpy ground, and tuk tuks are not the most stable of machines, a sudden change of direction in pursuit of the ball being almost enough to send them toppling over. While tuk tuks may not be as quick around the field as horses, at least nobody has to sweep up after them when the game is over.

Matches are made up of two seven-minute chukkas with a fifteen-minute half-time interval for refuelling both players and tuk tuks. To encourage a fast, open game, with plenty of bumper-to-bumper action, ultra-defensive tactics are forbidden – teams are not allowed to park a tuk tuk in front of the goal to stop their opponents scoring. No team may have more than two of its tuk tuks in one half of the field at any given time and only one tuk tuk from each team is allowed to enter the goalmouth D zone. A foul is declared if a player hooks an opponent's stick or if a tuk tuk is deliberately parked or driven over the ball to prevent the opposing team reaching it. Running over an opponent's mallet is also considered bad sportsmanship. According to the official website: 'Gentlemen may only play with their right hand, ladies may use both hands. In the event of a dispute about a player's sex, the umpire's decision will be final.'

TURKEY BOWLING, INTERNATIONAL FALLS, MINNESOTA, USA

The sport of turkey bowling truly is poultry in motion. It is just like ordinary ten-pin bowling except that instead of a ball a 12-pound frozen turkey is bowled at the pins and instead of a gutterball you have a butterball.

It is believed to have been invented in 1988 by Derrick Johnson, a clerk at a grocery store in Newport Beach, California, who, late one night, saw a manager slide a frozen turkey across the floor and accidentally knock over a soda bottle. Johnson was instantly inspired and devised a game to be played in supermarket aisles with frozen turkeys and ten plastic soft drinks bottles. He became the self-appointed commissioner of the Poultry Bowlers Association and created a set of rules and terminology such as the 'fowl line' (foul line), a 'gobbler' (three strikes in a row), a 'hen' (a spare) and a 'wishbone' (a 7–10 split). A former Chippendales dancer, Johnson had visions of developing a supermarket Olympics featuring turkey bowling to raise money for the poor. 'This is the sport of the nineties,' he predicted to the *Los Angeles Times*. 'I can see it now. The party invitation will read: BYOB – Bring Your Own Bird.'

Although the sport has maybe yet to scale the heights Johnson had hoped for, it has become a feature of North American Thanksgiving celebrations and, when played on ice, as a sideshow at minor league ice hockey games. It is also a popular event at the annual Icebox Days festival in International Falls, Minnesota, a celebration of all things wintry, where frozen turkeys are bowled at a set of pins along an ice lane marked with spray paint.

Protestors argue that turkey bowling is disrespectful to animals and while they certainly have a case, one suspects that if the turkey had a say it might well raise a greater objection to being frozen in the first place. Even so, when the first UK Turkey Bowling Championships were staged in Manchester in 2003, the organisers were forced to use plastic turkeys after animal rights campaigners had told them in no uncertain terms to get stuffed.

UNICYCLE FOOTBALL, SAN MARCOS, TEXAS, USA

Unicycle football is similar to American football except – and the clue here is in the name – it is played on unicycles. Its stronghold is the Texas city of San Marcos, where it was invented in 2008 by juggler Marcus Garland – aka Larry Gunn – who managed to convince enough friends that unicycle football was not as daft as it sounds. His faith was soon rewarded with the formation of the Unicycle Football League, which has eight teams from the area that play every Sunday in a fifty-six-game season.

There are usually five unicyclists on each team (although there can be as many as eleven depending on the size of the playing area), and each rider wears a helmet and carries a flag. As the field is a hard surface such as a car park, to minimise the risk of injury you can tackle an opponent simply by pulling their flag. This is the preferred method, but the alternative way of tackling is to knock your opponent off his unicycle with 'the least amount of force required to cause the ball handler to dismount their unicycle'. Determining precisely how much force constitutes 'the least amount required' is very much open to individual interpretation, meaning that the rule does not stop riders from hurling themselves into tackles and sending opposing unicyclists flying. Many a play ends up with a pile of twisted frames and spinning wheels. Kicking the ball requires an acrobatic mid-swing dismount, which could easily lead a novice to do himself a mischief, while riders regularly launch themselves out of the saddle to catch high passes since receiving team players are allowed to get off their unicycle to catch the ball. However, a pass can only be made while on the unicycle. Penalties are awarded for such infringements as blocking, holding, unnecessary roughness, kicking out with intent, and 'indecent touching', which is apparently a form of blocking.

Instead of a boring old coin toss, the game starts with an entertaining unicycle battle where two riders joust using long bamboo sticks with a boxing glove on the end. Whoever wins the joust by causing his opponent to dismount gets to choose whether his team kicks or receives. Surely this is the way forward for other sports. Think how much more exhilarating a frame break at snooker would be if the players fought each other to the brink of death with their cues.

The season's showpiece event is called the Stupor Bowl, complete with cheerleaders and a half-time show featuring a lone bagpiper or a band rolled out on a flatbed trailer. 'We try to make the Stupor Bowl sound bigger than it really is,' admits Garland, 'and I think we succeed.' Speaking to reporter Bill Bowman, he added: 'It's a beer-drinking sport. If you're going home and lifting weights to play unicycle football, you're playing the wrong sport. This is about drinking beer and partying and having a good time with your friends.'

It may have been created as a fun game, but the skill of the players should not be underestimated, because if you think throwing a football with a degree of accuracy is difficult, try doing it while perched on a unicycle.

CHAPTER THREE

TRIVIAL PURSUITS

CANAL JUMPING, FRIESLAND, THE NETHERLANDS

Of all the things you can do on a canal, vaulting over one by means of a long pole would not come high on many people's lists. Not unless they were from the Dutch province of Friesland, where canal jumping – or *fierljeppen* – has become the national sport of the Frisian people. Recent figures indicate that there are over five hundred registered canal jumpers in the world, almost half from the Netherlands.

The sport dates back to the eighteenth century when it was practised by farmers who used poles to jump over drainage channels so that they could reach otherwise inaccessible plots of land. However, it was not until 1957 that it was properly structured. Participants originally used wooden poles before graduating first to aluminium and recently to carbon, which are tough and stiff but extremely lightweight meaning they fall more slowly. The poles used in competition are between twenty-six and forty-three feet long (longer poles equate to greater distances) and have a round flat plate at the base to prevent them from sinking into the mud at the bottom of the canal. Competitors run up to the pole (*polsstok*), which is positioned vertically in the water towards the canal's nearside bank, leap through the air, then grab it and climb up it as quickly as they can while using their weight to tip it to the other side. If they have managed to control the forward movement and restrict the lateral movement of the pole successfully, it will dump them in a sand pit on the far side of the canal. If they have been less successful, it will dump them in the water. Similarly, if they are unable to ascend the pole quickly enough, the ensuing lack of forward momentum will almost certainly result in a soaking. To provide the extra grip needed to climb the slippery pole, competitors strap rubber bicycle inner tubes to their feet. There may not be much demand for conventional climbing equipment in the Netherlands, but there is never a shortage of bicycle tyres.

Successful jumps are then measured at the point where the vaulter landed in the sand. In 2011, Bart Helmholt set a new world record of 21.51 metres at the Dutch Championships and promptly celebrated by jumping into the very canal he had fought so hard to avoid. There are over one hundred and fifty events on the *fierljeppen* calendar. These run throughout the summer months, with the national championships taking place in August. The 2012 champion, data analyst Oane Galama, has perfected his own idiosyncratic canal-jumping style. 'It's a special technique, which places emphasis on the dismount. You have to try and propel yourself as far as possible at the peak of the pole. You have to swing your legs up and your arms go back. You then use the momentum to spring off the pole. It's a good technique, but not one that many jumpers can control.'

One of the leading women jumpers, Kimberly Engelhard, says: 'As long as you let go at the right time and fall well, it's not dangerous. But you have to pay attention to what you are doing. Every jump is different. The weather changes, and there's the wind to contend with. You always want to take risks and jump further – that's the beauty of the sport.'

The other beauty of *fierljeppen* is its high potential for acute embarrassment. If sliding down the pole and being dunked in the water is not bad enough, pity the poor competitors who sprint along the approach, leap through the air and then miss the pole altogether, ending up straight in the water. That is the equivalent of a jockey missing his horse. But do they care? Well, yes, they do a bit.

CHAP OLYMPIAD, LONDON, ENGLAND

Founded in 1999 by Gustav Temple, *The Chap* is a bimonthly magazine that takes a wry look at the modern world through the steamed-up monocle of a more refined age. Championing the rights of that most endangered of species, the English gentleman, it evokes an era of cucumber sandwiches, afternoon tea and hat doffing, where manners and sartorial elegance ruled the day. *The Chap* firmly believes that a society without courteous behaviour and proper headwear is a society on the brink of collapse. As such it is very much at odds with the vulgarity of the twenty-first century.

Nowhere is this view more apparent than in the field of sport. *The Chap* has no time for the win-at-all-costs attitude of the modern Olympics; instead it glories in that noblest of creatures, the gallant British loser, for whom the taking part and dignity in inevitable defeat were all that mattered. *The Chap* remembers when the scoring of a goal at football warranted nothing more than a brisk congratulatory handshake instead of the painstakingly choreographed – and appallingly executed – routines that blight the game today.

Seeking an event to showcase its sporting ethos, in 2005 the magazine staged the first Chap Olympiad, a tribute to eccentricity on the field of play that has proved so popular it is now held every July in Bedford Square Gardens in the Bloomsbury area of London. According to its mission statement, the Chap Olympiad is 'a celebration of Britain's sporting ineptitude, providing track, field and bar events for the floppy of hair, the rakish of trilby and the elegant of trouser ... where sensational cravats take precedence over sweaty Lycra and more points are awarded for maintaining immaculate trouser creases than crossing the finishing line.' It is a sporting gathering where everyone has a stiff upper lip, even if it is usually concealed by a lavish moustache.

Only the most athletically challenged – 'the frail of form and the fearful of sport' – are invited to don their tweeds, posh frocks and pearls to compete. Everyone turns up wearing outfits from the 1920s to the 1950s: any form of modern sportswear results in instant disqualification. The opening ceremony begins with the lighting of the Olympic pipe and although the programme of events changes from year to year, if you're lucky you may be able to witness, or take part in, quill throwing (where a quill is thrown at a target while poetry is read aloud), iron board surfing, the cucumber sandwich discus, beach volleybowler (where the ball is replaced with a bowler hat), the tug o'hair, and necktie kwando. Physical activity is kept to a minimum, although those who like the element of danger in their sport will not be disappointed by the umbrella jousting contest, in which two chaps wearing bowler hats and riding bicycles engage in mild combat with their umbrellas.

More sedate affairs include the pipeathlon, where competitors complete a lap or two around the running track at a leisurely pace while carrying a fully lit pipe, and the hop, skip and a G&T, where chapettes hop, skip and jump holding a full glass of gin and tonic. In keeping with the spirit of the afternoon, the winner is not the one who covers the greatest distance but the one left with the most drink in their glass. Another event to look out for is the three-trousered limbo, in which couples share an outsize pair of trousers, run to a limbo pole and try to pass under it. The trousers must remain at a discreet level throughout, with points deducted for underwear revelation. One of the most keenly contested games is bounders, in which chaps must say something so caddish to a lady that he receives a slap, the one with the reddest face being the winner. Teamwork comes to the fore in the martini knockout relay, where teams compete to mix the perfect dry martini over a gruelling ten-yard course, with the handicap of having no butler to do it for them.

The Chap Olympiad harks back to a more innocent time when 30-love was not an orgy, a face-off was not a cosmetic procedure and the only drugs used in sport were an extra pinch of snuff.

HAKA PEI, EASTER ISLAND

Easter Island in the South Pacific is best known for its giant stone statues, more than a thousand of which are mysteriously scattered across the landscape. But for the connoisseur of sporting weirdness, the island houses an equally puzzling diversion by the name of Haka Pei. If you have ever longed to see young men ride a giant banana log at speed down a steep hill while virtually naked, then Easter Island is most definitely the place to visit.

Haka Pei is a sporting event where a dozen or so competitors demonstrate their courage and foolhardiness by tobogganing down the side of an extinct volcano on two six-foot-long banana tree trunks. The two trunks are positioned side by side and lashed together with twine, an angled cut being made in the front of the trunks to attain greater speed. The slope on the 300-foot-high Maunga Pui hill – the island's steepest incline – is forty-five degrees, and the riders lie down and descend feet first as in a luge. The rider who travels the greatest distance without falling off is declared the winner. Bearing in mind that speeds of over 40mph can be reached and that the transport of choice offers no protection whatsoever, you might expect safety clothing to be in order in the form of a helmet and padding. But these islanders are made of stronger stuff. Instead they strip naked, add some body paint, a few feathers and a discreetly placed loin covering, and hurtle down pretty much as nature intended. Quite apart from the speed, the logs have no steering and are impossible to manoeuvre, meaning that there is a reasonable chance of ending up in bushes or trees. One Western visitor reported that the first three competitors he saw were carted off in an ambulance. Even those who don't need medical treatment are usually covered in bruises by the end of the run.

Haka Pei is part of Easter Island's Tapati festival, which began in 1975 as a way of promoting local Polynesian culture. It runs for the first two weeks of February and includes a number of diverse events. Among the other sporting highlights are eel catching, body surfing and the Tapati Rapa Nui, a triathlon run inside the crater of the thankfully extinct Rano Raraku volcano. The competitors start by paddling across a lagoon inside the crater in small canoes made of reed. They then hang a 55-pound bundle of bananas around their necks and, carrying their fruity load, run a complete lap around the lagoon. Finally, they climb on small reed floats and swim back across the lake – all in 80-degree heat. Something tells me these intrepid young men might not find the egg-and-spoon race much of a challenge.

HIDE AND SEEK WORLD CHAMPIONSHIP, ITALY

Although the official event dates back only to 2010, many historians argue that the first true hide and seek world champions were the crew of the *Mary Celeste*. One hundred and forty-five years on and they still haven't been found. That is world-class hiding.

The Nascondino World Championship, as it is known (*nascondino* being Italian for 'hide and seek'), was devised by a small magazine after an adults' birthday party. One of the creators, Simone Montanari, told sputniknews.com: 'Once we celebrated my birthday and began to play hide and seek as when we were children. I was struck by a brilliant idea: why not organise a hide and seek international championship?' It started out as a one-off caper in Bergamo but it proved so popular that it has turned into an annual affair, even awarding itself world championship status. Since it is for groups of five adults who have to pay around £100 per team to enter, the rules are a little more complex than the familiar childhood version, although traditionalists will be relieved to know that the seekers still have to count to sixty before setting off in pursuit of their quarry.

The teams are split into four groups and one person in each group hides while a 'neutral searching team' made up of agile rugby and American football players counts out the sixty seconds. The hidden player then has ten minutes to emerge from their hiding place and reach a mattress located in the middle of a huge field before any of the searchers manages either to find them or apprehend them. This is no easy task as the neutral searchers are fast runners and strong tacklers, so simply jumping out of a hiding place and attempting to out-run them across the field is not the wisest move. It is a contest that calls for guile and cunning but as it still often ends in a frantic race across the field between hider and seekers, the mattress used is soft enough to cushion a desperate dive. Participants stress the importance of strategy, with the key decision being when exactly to emerge from the hiding place and take a chance across the open field. Subtle camouflage is obviously an option, but the searchers are sure to be wise to moving hay bales or cows that walk upright on two legs. A hider who fails to evade the seekers or does not reach the target mattress within the time limit earns no points. The rules are strictly enforced by two referees and a co-ordinator. At the end of the two days, the team with most points is declared World Hide and Seek champions.

At the 2016 event, sixty-four teams from Italy, France, Belgium, Switzerland and the USA tried to outwit each other over two days to win the coveted Golden Fig Leaf. That year's competition was staged in the northern village of Consonno, which was once a thriving tourist spot but, following a 1976 landslide that blocked access, has now become a ghost town. With so many abandoned buildings offering refuge, it was deemed an ideal venue for a large-scale game of hide and seek. As word spread about the championships, members of Japan's Olympic committee actually considered including a version of hide and seek in the 2020 Games. Alas, in the end the sport has not been selected for inclusion. It can only be a matter of time, however, before hide and seek calls to the Olympics loud and clear: 'Coming!'

INTERNATIONAL BOGNOR BIRDMAN, BOGNOR
REGIS, WEST SUSSEX, ENGLAND

First held in 1971, the International Birdman contest celebrates the pre-Wright Brothers days when men believed that they could fly by strapping a large pair of wings to their bodies and taking a giant leap into the unknown. The only difference is that at the International Birdman it is not a leap into the unknown but a leap into the English Channel . . . off a pier.

Devised by former RAF photographer George Abel, it was known originally as the International Birdman Rally and was staged at Selsey with a prize of £1,000 going to anyone who could fly a distance of fifty yards, a feat that proved beyond everyone. In 1978, the organisers were told they could no longer use the pier at Selsey and the event was moved along the coast to Bognor Regis, but in 2008 work on Bognor pier saw the intrepid birdmen take off at Worthing instead. For a few years, birdman competitions were staged in both Worthing and Bognor, but after the 2015 event, Worthing flew the nest due to escalating costs.

Competitors run off an elevated ramp at the end of the pier and there is a large cash prize to anyone who flies 100 metres. When legendary ski jumper Eddie 'The Eagle' Edwards had a go in 1989, he managed just eleven metres before splashdown. The current Bognor Birdman record of 89.2 metres was set in 1992 by a local man, Dave Bradshaw. While some view the event as a chance to test their homemade flying machines, the less serious aviators simply want to dress up. Entrants have included a pantomime horse, Donald Duck, a flying squirrel, a magic carpet, Dr Who, a skateboarding cow, and the Pope. These rarely manage more than a few metres before receiving a soaking.

The Worthing event attracted controversy in 2009 when forty-seven-year-old Steve Elkins, from Derbyshire, flew 99.86 metres, thus tantalisingly missing out on the big money prize even though he claimed that video footage showed he had exceeded the distance. Elkins said he felt cheated. There was further acrimony in 2013 after experienced Northumberland birdman Ron Freeman spent an unprecedented seventeen seconds in the air and flew 141.5 metres, only to be denied the prize because he had taken advantage of strong winds to fly sideways off the pier rather than forwards. However, there were no arguments at the 2014 event when Freeman flew 159.8 metres in his adapted hang-glider the *Geordie Flyer*. 'I feel like I've won the lottery,' he said of his £10,000 prize, which was seen as a fitting reward for someone who had been fearlessly hurling himself off the piers of West Sussex and plunging into the sea for sixteen years.

KITE BATTLE, SANJO, JAPAN

In the West, kites chiefly provide simple pleasures, fluttering prettily high in the sky, but in parts of Asia they cut a more sinister sight when the lines are fitted with razor blades, sharp knives or broken glass for the merciless pursuit of kite fighting. Thus an innocent childhood pastime is turned into a blood sport, like manufacturing skipping ropes from barbed wire or filling conkers with dynamite.

The kite skins are generally made from thin paper stretched over bamboo spars, but the lines are then sharpened menacingly with a coating comprising a mixture of finely crushed glass and rice glue. Alternatively, some fighters prefer metal lines while others attach knives or blades to the line or to the actual kite. There is a great deal of skill involved in kite fighting, for the flyers need to use tactics and the prevailing winds to cut their opponent's line and win the contest. In multiple kite-fighting matches, the person with the last kite in the air after all the others have been ripped to shreds is declared the winner. Another discipline is the capture competition, which is like aerial wrestling for kites. Competitors use their kites to try to slice through their opponent's line and then encircle the trailing line of the cut kite. By doing this, the victor is deemed to have captured the other kite and is able to fly both kites at the same time. The contest is over when the vanquished kite is grounded.

One of the biggest and oldest kite fights in Japan is the Sanjo Great Kite Battle, which takes place on the first weekend in June. Kite fighting in Sanjo originated around the seventeenth century when, after seeing the children from military camps flying their kites, the local blacksmith's children craftily used their own kites to cut the others in mid-air. Thereafter it developed into a battle between the children of the wealthy and the children of common-ers, but before long, adults muscled in on the fun and it became an annual event. Kites in Sanjo tend to be hexagonal rather than rectangular. Over the years, communities within the city began competing against each other. Now around twenty teams take part in the two-day Sanjo Great Kite Battle, or *Ika Gassen*, for which the kites are painted with pictures of medieval Japanese warriors and flown from the Sanjo Disaster Prevention Centre in re-enactments of famous bygone military conflicts.

The battleground is divided into two halves, for red and white teams. One point is awarded for entangling and causing an oppo-nent's kite to fall, three points for cutting in mid-air, and five points for an outstanding cut in mid-air as ruled by the judges. The results are based on the total team scores over the two days. Pre-battle training is alarmingly intense – almost to military level – and sometimes means forgoing sleep. During the battle, tempers can become frayed if rival kite fighters get too close on the ground. In 2016, the East Sanjo Satsuki team became the first to win the title for six consecutive years.

Kite fighting may be revered in Japan, but in Pakistan it was banned in 2007 following as many as eleven kite-related deaths that year. Kite flyers were reported to be concentrating so hard that they accidentally fell off rooftops while others were electro-cuted when their kites made contact with overhead power lines. Meanwhile, the glass-coated lines used to cut rival kites had occa-sionally sliced through the necks of innocent bystanders and motorcyclists, causing horrific injuries and even the odd fatality. As a result, some riders fitted their bikes with arched rods to protect against the deadly kites. To reduce the risk of accidents, the Lahore Kite Flying Association proposed creating designated kite-flying zones, but police have continued to arrest fighters and confiscate their kites. Most are released fairly quickly but, as you might expect with kite flyers, there are strings attached: any future transgression could result in a jail sentence. Who would have thought a kite could ever be classed as an offensive weapon?

POLE SITTING, FRIESLAND, THE NETHERLANDS

It has to be said: pole sitting is not as popular as it used to be. Part of the problem is that the world record, set by St Simeon Stylites the Elder who, in an attempt to be nearer to God, spent thirty-seven years on top of a stone pillar in Syria right up until his death in AD 459, is unlikely ever to be broken. Even the keenest pole sitter would baulk at spending half their life up there.

The golden age of pole sitting was the 1920s. American stunt actor and former sailor Alvin 'Shipwreck' Kelly made a third career out of sitting on the top of a pole for hours, days and even weeks on end. In 1924, he came down after thirteen hours and thirteen minutes, but his feat merely served to inspire a raft of imitators, who managed to extend the world record to twenty-one days. In 1929, Kelly decided to reclaim his record and perched atop a flagpole in Atlantic City, New Jersey for forty-nine days, only to see his achievement surpassed the following year by Bill Penfield, who sat on a flagpole in Iowa for over fifty-one days until he was forced down by a thunderstorm, which, along with territorial seagulls and incontinent pigeons, is an occupational hazard for pole sitters.

Another American showman, Richard 'Dixie' Blandy, took up the challenge, and in 1964 sat for seventy-eight days on the top of a pole in Atlantic City. Blandy was fiercely protective of his accomplishment and, as others broke his record, he dismissed their claims because they had constructed elaborate sitting platforms whereas he continued to use nothing more than a small seat. His view – and an excellent one it was from the top of a pole – was that there should be no luxuries for the dedicated pole sitter. Alas, his pole-sitting career came to an untimely end in 1974 when he died at the age of seventy-two after the Chicago flagpole on which he was sitting collapsed without warning.

Daniel Baraniuk, an unemployed twenty-seven-year-old from Gdansk, Poland, set the modern world record for pole sitting by perching on top of an eight-foot-two-and-half-inch-high pole for 196 days and nights to win the 2002 World Pole-Sitting Championship and nearly $23,000 in prize money. The competitors mounted their poles at a fun park in Soltau, Northern Germany on 15 May and were only permitted to leave the sixteen-inch by twenty-four-inch platform for ten minutes every two hours. Baraniuk finally gave up on 26 November, his closest rival having fallen off the pole a month earlier.

Although the world championships seem to have temporarily fallen by the wayside, there is an endurance pole-sitting competition in the Netherlands called *paalzitten*. As we have seen from canal jumping, people in the Friesland region of the country are very keen on doing things with poles. The sport arose from the practice of Dutch canal boat hands who used to rest on the canalside poles that are used to moor barges. It has also been suggested that Frieslanders thought pole sitting would relieve the boredom of the long winter months, but it fell out of favour when they realised that sitting on a pole was actually more boring than the long winter months. Happily, the sport has enjoyed a revival in recent years, and as the poles are erected in water, competitors don't get hurt when they fall off.

Since 1994, the Dutch island of Aruba in the Caribbean has hosted an annual *paalzitten* contest in the capital, Oranjestad, that can last for what must seem like an eternity, the sitters' only relief being a toilet break every few hours. At the 2012 event, Liesbeth Cornes and another islander, Shurman Milliard, eventually shared first place with a time of eighty-seven hours fifty-two minutes. Imagine sitting on a pole for nearly four days and nights and finding that you haven't even won outright!

Meanwhile pole-related events in Britain are pretty much confined to the **UK Pole Climbing Championships** and Miss Pole Dance UK. It is considered unusual for anyone to enter both competitions.

REDNECK GAMES, BEAVERTON, MICHIGAN, USA

When the Olympics were awarded to Atlanta in 1996, some of the media remarked disparagingly that the Games were going to be run by a bunch of rednecks. Local DJ Mac Davis took mild exception to this and, to reinforce the stereotype, organised the first Redneck Games in East Dublin, Georgia. 'If that's what they want, let's give it to them,' he said.

It has been said that the definition of a redneck is someone whose bathroom deodoriser is a box of matches, whose wedding takes place in the delivery room, whose dog serves as a dishwasher, and whose family tree does not fork. Rednecks are depicted as good ole country boys who own a home that is mobile and five cars that aren't. They are high on having fun, low on having teeth, and love beer, trucks and women – in that order. As one of their ilk summed it up: 'A redneck works hard, plays hard, and dies broke.'

Billed as 'more fun than indoor plumbing', the 1996 Redneck Games opened with its own unique take on the traditional athletes' parade, at which the propane torch was decorated with aluminium from a six-pack of Budweiser. Events included typical redneck pastimes such as the mud pit belly flop (as ungainly as it sounds), watermelon seed spitting, the cigarette flip, hubcap hurling, dumpster diving, and the toilet seat horseshoe toss. There was also a game where competitors had to bob for pigs' trotters. One enthusiast explained the technique involved: 'You have to dive head first into the water, push the trotter to the bottom of the bowl using your face, and then bite as hard as you can on the trotter while pulling your head back out.' Another hotly contested event was the armpit serenade. Davis said: 'That's when you cup your hand under your armpit and make farting noises or tunes.'

At the 1998 Redneck Games, one competitor pumped out the entire theme tune to the TV series *Green Acres*. And in each case, the winners received as a trophy an empty, half-crushed, mounted can of beer.

An estimated five thousand people turned out for the first Redneck Games – over twice the population of East Dublin – and, tempted by copious amounts of beer and tasty redneck snacks such as fried alligator on a stick, this figure soon rose to fifteen thousand. 'The fact that it is not politically correct has made the event popular,' Davis told the *Chicago Tribune* in 2001. 'The great thing about being Southern is that we have a sense of humour and are able to laugh at ourselves.' But eventually the joke started to wear thin and interest waned to the extent that in 2013 the Games were cancelled. However, the concept has not been lost. Canada staged its own Redneck Games in Minto, Ontario, for five years from 2006 (adding mud pit tug-of-war and mud pit volleyball to the itinerary), and in 2014, a fresh celebration of redneck sports culture started up in Beaverton, Michigan. Like Ontario, this is a long way from traditional redneck country. Nevertheless, many of the original events have continued to flourish in Michigan, embellished by such pursuits as grape stomping, chicken-shit bingo (an avian variation on cow-pat bingo) and a cardboard boat race. It is especially gratifying to report that the toilet seat horseshoe toss, in which competitors must throw a toilet seat over a distant peg, is still going strong. Apparently, the key to success in the event is to ensure that a redneck is not sitting on the toilet seat at the time.

SHIN KICKING WORLD CHAMPIONSHIPS, DOVER'S HILL, CHIPPING CAMPDEN, GLOUCESTERSHIRE, ENGLAND

Anyone who has sat opposite a toddler on a bus will know that some people are born shin kickers. It just comes naturally to them, like putting sticky fingers on shiny surfaces and getting chocolate on a new white shirt. However, not all are able to carry on perfecting their art into adulthood, which is why the annual Shin Kicking World Championships performs such a valuable social and sporting function.

In a nutshell, shin kicking is a sport in which competitors take it in turns to kick each other in the lower leg until one of them falls over. But there is more to it than that. Event chairman Graham Greenall explained to the *Daily Mirror*: 'It takes a great tolerance of pain but you also need to be agile and you need to be fit. It's quite skilful. There are rules. You can only kick between the ankle and the shin, and it has to be a fair trip; you kick somebody, you take their leg out, but you can't just push them over.'

Derived from Cumberland wrestling, shin kicking dates back to the seventeenth century. It used to be a brutal sport that produced serious injuries until steel-capped boots were banned. One observer wrote of it: 'There is no imbecility nor barbarity that human beings will not practise and even exalt, so long as it be sanctified by custom.' In olden days, competitors would try to increase their pain threshold by means of a strict training regime that involved whacking their own shins with wooden mallets. Nowadays shin kickers wear softer shoes and, in a bid to lessen the impact of repeated kicks, they stuff straw down their socks. But this padding can become dislodged in the heat of combat, leaving flesh and bone dangerously exposed to the next assault. So the more nimble competitors turn their bodies to try and make sure that their opponents' kicks land on the fleshier sides of the leg.

Combatants stand face to face and, holding on to each other's collar, aim blows at their opponent's shin with the inside of the foot or the toes. Only in mid-kick can a player attempt to bring his opponent to the ground. A shin has to be kicked before a fall can be scored. The matches are decided on a best-of-three basis, with the official judge, or stickler, who traditionally wears a white coat similar to a shepherd's smock, determining whether falls are legitimate. Any combatant who feels he has suffered enough can surrender by calling 'sufficient'. The victor progresses to the next round, the eventual champion being quite literally the last man standing. But even he will be walking with a limp for the next few days.

The Shin Kicking World Championships are the showpiece event in the Cotswold Olimpicks, a series of rural sporting pursuits originally created by lawyer Robert Dover in 1612. Even though crowds of 30,000 regularly gathered on the hill named after him in the early nineteenth century, their rowdy, bawdy behaviour led for calls for the Olimpicks to be banned. The local rector of the time, Rev. Geoffrey Drinkwater Bourne, claimed that 'from 1846 onwards, the games, instead of being as they were originally intended to be decorously conducted, became the trysting place of all the lowest scum of the population which lived in the districts lying between Birmingham and Oxford'.

They were eventually discontinued in 1852, only to be revived annually from 1965. The Olimpicks now take place on the Friday after Spring Bank Holiday – in early June. The more dangerous sports of the past, such as fighting with swords and cudgels, have been replaced by the likes of wheelbarrow racing, sledgehammer throwing, piano smashing, and spurning the barre, a Cotswold version of tossing the caber.

But it is the shin kicking that everyone wants to win, even though the combatants really suffer for their sport. 'It's very, very painful,' said one. 'In fact it's not just for the first day. The first time I did it, it was six months before my legs stopped being painful.' Small wonder, then, that it is quite rare for champions to return the following year to defend their title. This is a world championship that is constantly up for grabs.

UK ROCK PAPER SCISSORS CHAMPIONSHIPS, LONDON, ENGLAND

It has long been suggested that, instead of engaging in calamitous military conflict, the ideal way for nations to settle disputes would be a game of Rock Paper Scissors. Equally, if two men are fighting over the same woman, forget the expensive flowers, jewellery or caravan weekends in Ingoldmells; just sort it by a quick game of Rock Paper Scissors. And if either suitor thinks that is somehow trivialising the relationship and their level of commitment to the lady, make it best of three.

Although similar hand games were commonplace in China over 2,000 years ago, the modern form of Rock Paper Scissors probably derives from *jan-ken*, a Japanese game that was popular in the nineteenth century. As Japanese contact with the West increased, the game spread to Europe and in 1842 the Paper Scissors Stone Club was founded in London. It stated: 'The club is dedicated to the exploration and dissemination of knowledge regarding the game of Paper Scissors Stone and providing a safe legal environment for the playing of said game.' In 1918, its name was changed to the World Rock Paper Scissors (RPS) Club and its headquarters moved to Canada. By the mid-1920s, it had enough active members – an estimated ten thousand worldwide – to stage an official championship. Canada became very much a hotbed of the game, regularly staging an RPS World Championships in the early years of the twenty-first century, but although that event was last staged in 2009, the UK Rock Paper Scissors Championships, which were first held in 2007, have continued to prosper.

Organised by entertainment company Wacky Nation, the Championships attract 150 competitors to the Green Man pub in the Bank area of London in November, each hoping to battle their way through seven rounds of intense hand shaping to be declared UK champion and win a first prize of £100. In keeping with the sponsor's USP, players are encouraged to wear fancy dress. In fact, among the handy tips experts suggest is wearing a scissors or rock-themed costume and then throwing paper to fool your opponent. They also recommend wearing sunglasses to prevent your opponent from studying your eyes. Another cunning tactic is to shout the name of one move before throwing another, although this does reek of extreme gamesmanship.

The rules are simple. The players stand at either side of a table, shake hands, then count one, two, and throw their move on three. In elite RPS circles, this is known as Priming the Chump. Rock beats scissors, scissors beats paper, paper beats rock. No other weapons – such as grenade – are recognised in the UK game.

However, the Rock Paper Scissors devotee should be wary when chancing his arm abroad for fear of falling foul of local variations. In Malaysia, for example, they play Stone, Water, Bird. Bird, which is represented by the five fingertips brought together to form a beak, beats water (an open palm) by drinking it, stone beats bird by hitting it, and water beats stone, because the stone sinks in it.

In the end, whatever the moves, it all boils down to psyching out the opposition, but some prefer to let fate deal its hand. 'My technique is not to have a technique,' explains one UK enthusiast. 'They won't see it coming, because I won't see it coming.'

UNDERWATER KISSING CHAMPIONSHIPS, SHANGHAI, CHINA

The growing sport of underwater kissing is not for everyone. In particular, it is not for people who don't like being underwater and who don't like kissing. If we're being honest, there are likely to be more of the former than the latter, but if you do like your kisses long and wet, Shanghai is the place to go.

The Underwater Kissing Championships are held annually in the city's Playa Maya Water Park to celebrate International Kissing Day (6 July). A total of fifteen couples took part in the 2016 contest, their goal being to see who could disappear beneath the surface and hold the kiss the longest without needing to come up for breath. Participants must be totally submerged for the kiss to count. A strong pair of lungs and a fondness for your kissing cohort are generally considered to offer the best chance of victory, and, let's face it, what could be more romantic than staring into someone's goggles while the sterile smell of chlorine fills your nostrils? The winning kiss has been known to last around one minute twenty seconds, which, by anyone's standards, constitutes prolonged puckering.

China is certainly the home of underwater kissing, and other similar events are staged across the country to mark Valentine's Day, including one in a huge aquarium, where the kissing divers don scuba gear and keep a watch out for sharks and sea urchins. Indeed, the Chinese seem obsessed with kissing competitions and merrily stage a wide variety of endurance kissing events on dry land, not only for couples but also for complete strangers. In Jilin in 2012, eighteen couples and their 'close friends' took part in a contorted-position kissing competition, where one couple twisted their torsos and locked lips for a staggering thirty minutes. At this rate, it can surely only be a matter of time before the Chinese transfer competitive kissing to a paddy field for an annual bog snog.

WORLD FLOUNDER TRAMPING CHAMPIONSHIPS, PALNACKIE, DUMFRIES AND GALLOWAY, SCOTLAND

Many methods of catching wild creatures for food have disappeared down the centuries. Sabre-tooth tiger hunting is one that readily springs to mind. Dodo netting is another. But flounder tramping has survived for thousands of years as an ingenious way of hooking fish with your toes.

Just as history has failed to chronicle who first thought an egg was a suitable thing to eat, nobody knows who first stepped barefoot on a flounder and concluded that this was the future of fishing. But for centuries, people have taken off their shoes and waded into the shallow waters of the Urr estuary in Dumfries and Galloway in the hope of locating a tasty flat fish beneath their toes. For when the tide goes out, the flounder, too lazy to swim out to sea, obligingly lies on the bottom of the estuary and buries itself in the mud, relying on its camouflage for protection. It obviously decided upon this strategy as a safeguard from marauding sea birds, but had reckoned without the sensitive human sole.

Veteran flounder-tramper John Kirk conceived the World Flounder Tramping Championships in 1973 to settle a pub wager as to who could catch the biggest flounder in the river estuary. Rods, lines and nets are conspicuous by their absence in this fishing competition with a difference, as the barefoot hopefuls venture chest-high into the water at low tide. Praying for a shortage of crabs, they step slowly through the mud until they feel the tell-tale wriggling of a flounder beneath their toes, at which point they pull the fish from the depths using manual dexterity, making this the only sport where 'fish fingers' is a medical condition. The captured flounder is then put into a plastic bag, or in some extreme cases, the tramper's swimming trunks. The flounder must be alive at the weigh-in, with whoever has caught the heaviest fish being declared World Flounder Tramping Champion.

Successful tramping depends entirely on feel because the water is so murky it is impossible to see more than an inch or two below the surface. It is important to move softly, lifting the foot a few inches clear of the mud before setting it down again. If you hurry or lose balance, the fish swim off. Experienced tramper Robbie Cowan admits that the first time you step on a flounder it can be as startling for the tramper as it is for the fish. 'A big one feels like a thick, slimy sponge,' he told *The Field*, 'and the rough spine down the centre of their body can be pretty uncomfortable. There is always a certain amount of wriggling, but the extent depends where your foot lands. Tread on their head and they thrash about and the tail comes up to smack you on the back of the leg.' Conversely, if you happen to land on the tail, the flounder will usually wriggle free before you can pick it up. The best place to tread, therefore, is on the centre of the body, but even then, the foot must be kept firmly down because if you lift it by so much as a fraction, the flounder will be off. If you do manage to keep your foot steady, apparently the fish seems to accept its fate and freezes on the spot, allowing you to bend down and pick it up.

In the competition's heyday, several hundred flounder trampers would converge on the Urr from all over Britain as well as from Russia, China, Europe, Canada and the United States. The event was temporarily removed from the sporting calendar in 2008, partly on safety grounds. The traditional method of capturing the tramped flounder was to use a three-pronged spear called a leister, but when – after a six-year absence – the championships were revived in 2014 by Sam Paterson, landlord of the Glen Isle Inn in Palnackie, it was decided to dispense with the leister lest any competitors should accidentally spear their own feet. Even so,

Scottish animal rights activists called the revival an 'embarrassing step backwards' and criticised the sport for being essentially 'dancing on fish'. Which coincidentally will probably soon be the title of a new ITV Saturday night entertainment series.

WORLD POOH STICKS CHAMPIONSHIPS,
WITNEY, OXFORDSHIRE, ENGLAND

The great thing about pooh sticks is that it must be the cheapest, simplest sport in the world to play. You don't need an expensive set of clubs, boots or protective clothing; the only equipment required is a twig. Of course, there's nothing to stop you dressing up in helmet and shoulder pads or an all-in-one Lycra suit, but it might be considered a little over the top for dropping a piece of wood off a bridge and into the river below. That, basically, is pooh sticks. Two or more competitors simultaneously drop sticks into the water on the upstream side of a bridge, then run to the other side, and the one whose stick appears first on the downstream side of the bridge is the winner. It's all over in a couple of short, tense minutes.

The noble sport was invented by author A.A. Milne for his son Christopher Robin Milne and first featured in Milne's 1928 book *The House at Pooh Corner* when Winnie the Pooh accidentally dropped a pine cone into a river from a bridge and, delighted to see it appear on the other side, immediately devised the rules for pooh sticks. Milne originally played the game on Posingford Bridge in Ashdown Forest, East Sussex, a landmark which has subsequently been renamed Pooh Sticks Bridge. The old wooden bridge had to be rebuilt after being worn down by a multitude of tourists but the sport is still played there, although participants are advised to bring their own sticks because visitors have damaged many of the trees in the vicinity.

Despite the sport's Sussex roots, the World Pooh Sticks Championships have always been held in Oxfordshire, first on the River Thames and since 2015 on the Windrush at Witney. The event was started in 1984 by lockkeeper Lynn David at Day's Lock on the Thames as a means of raising funds for the Royal National Lifeboat Institution. He put out a box of sticks and a collection box and watched as people lobbed their sticks into the river from nearby Little Wittenham Bridge with such enthusiasm that it soon became an annual event, attracting as many as 700 participants every year, some from as far afield as Australia, the United States and Japan. However, the high volume of summer boat traffic on the Thames meant that the championships could only be held between October and March, leading to the postponement of the 2013 event due to severe flooding. So two years later, the River Windrush became the new home of pooh sticks.

The championships, which currently take place in early June, feature an individual competition and a six-person team event. The sticks used must be made of organic material, preferably willow. Nothing synthetic is permitted. All participants must hold their stick at arm's length and drop it at the same time on the referee's command. Taller competitors should lower their arm to the level of the shortest so that all sticks are released from the same height. Throwing is the great taboo of pooh sticks, and anyone judged to have deliberately thrown their stick into the river in the hope of gaining an advantage faces instant disqualification. Casual competitors are happy to leave the passage of their stick to chance, but seasoned pooh stickers try to locate the fastest-flowing section of river and drop there. However, the turbulence around the bridge supports means that it is difficult to predict the path that the individual sticks will take, so in the end, even if the winner insists otherwise, it is pretty much all down to luck. It is very much a sport for all ages, and world champions, who receive a trophy, have ranged from young children to adults old enough to know better but for whom this probably represents the pinnacle of their sporting achievement.

The World Pooh Sticks Championships were voted 'Britain's favourite quirky event' by readers of *Countryfile* magazine, and this seems to have encouraged certain city dwellers to develop urban pooh sticks. Instead of dropping twigs into the river, they deposit shopping trolleys.

WORLD STONE SKIMMING CHAMPIONSHIPS,
EASDALE ISLAND, ARGYLL, SCOTLAND

Easdale Island is the smallest permanently inhabited island of the Inner Hebrides. It was once the centre of the thriving Scottish slate-mining industry, and one of the disused quarries provides the ideal arena and materials for the World Stone Skimming Championships, held every year on the last Sunday in September. Although there is also an annual **All England Stone Skimming Championships** on Lake Windermere, it is the Argyll event that has awarded itself world status.

The championships were started in 1983 by Albert Baker but did not become a regular attraction until 1997 when they were resurrected by Easdale Island Community Development Group as a fundraising event. They now draw over three hundred international competitors of all ages, ranging from young boys and girls to the 'old tosser' category for senior skimmers. The world champion receives a cup while the Bertie, named after the event's founder, is presented to the Easdale Islander who skims the furthest.

Each competitor is allowed three skims using specially selected Easdale slate skimming stones that measure no more than three inches in diameter. For a stone to qualify, it must bounce at least three times on the surface of the water and stay within the designated lane as marked by a series of buoys. The stone is then judged on the distance achieved before it sinks. If it strikes the back wall of the quarry – 206 feet away – that is registered as the official distance, regardless of whether the stone may have continued considerably further. When more than one skimmer hits the wall, a tie-break follows in the form of a three-stone 'toss off'. In 2016, Scottish delivery driver Dougie Isaacs, who has been skimming stones for more than thirty-five years, after being taught by his grandfather, and who can skim a stone 350 feet, was crowned world champion for the eighth time, including four wins on the bounce. Isaacs likes to let his stones do the talking, but fellow competitor, Welsh veteran Ron Long, reckons there are two elements to successful stone skimming. 'The first is power,' he told STV News. 'The stone is not going any further than you project it. Secondly it comes down to a bit of technique. You have to get the first bounce right because then it becomes aerodynamically stable. That helps the spin, the angle, and again the power. Every time it hits the water, it slows down, and to get the distance Dougie managed, it will hit the water between twenty and thirty times. So you can imagine the power in it.'

Experts advise novice skimmers to choose flat, smooth stones, ideally with a potential finger notch that will help achieve maximum spin and keep the stone skimming. The stone should be released with a low enough trajectory to keep it flat and with sufficient power to make the stone spin but without compromising the technique.

Ron Long sees a bright future for competitive stone skimming. 'In the Olympics, they can get horses to do God knows what,' he says, presumably referring to dressage. 'Stone skimming could be developed worldwide. Every man and his dog skims stones.' Now there's a thought: the World Canine Stone Skimming Championships – no need for marker buoys, just use pointers.

WORLD WORM CHARMING CHAMPIONSHIPS, WILLASTON, CHESHIRE, ENGLAND

In 1979, John Bailey, deputy headmaster of Willaston County Primary School in Cheshire, had the idea of setting up a 10p-a-go worm-charming stall as an attraction at the school summer fete. It proved such a winner that what was intended to be a one-off quickly evolved into the World Worm Charming Championships, which have been held annually in the village since 1980. The person who lures the most worms to the surface in thirty minutes receives a trophy in the shape of a golden rampant worm. The consolation prize of the silver worm trophy goes to the competitor who charms the heaviest worm. It has grown into such an international event that the rules are now printed in over thirty languages, including Tibetan.

For the championships, the Worm Arena is divided into 144 squares, each measuring three metres square. Most competitors lure worms to the surface by hand-vibrating a four-tine garden fork inserted approximately fifteen centimetres into the turf – a method known as twanging – although others prefer to use cricket stumps or knitting needles or even to tap dance on a plank to the *Star Wars* theme. Any form of music can be used to encourage the worms to the surface. 'They like rock best,' Stan Allen, who has been known to serenade them with his guitar, told the *Daily Telegraph.* 'Easy listening doesn't do it for them, and classical puts them to sleep.'

Digging is strictly banned as is the use of water, which, for the purposes of worm charming, is considered an illegal stimulant. This followed a spate of unsavoury incidents where the water had been laced with washing-up liquid, which irritates the worm's skin and drives the poor creature to the surface. Competitors who do not wish to handle worms may appoint a second – or 'Gillie' – to do so, and to ensure that no worms are harmed in the pursuit of sport, the charmees are released that evening after the birds have gone to roost.

The inexperienced charmer may succumb to premature worm grasping, or PWG. This is the equivalent of an own goal at football or a double fault at tennis. Championship organiser and Chief Wormer Mike Forster explains: 'It normally affects children under five and women over forty and is the name given when the charmer grabs the worm too early. It can result in one of two things happening: the worm going back underground and not coming out again, or a tug of worm, which invariably ends with the worm being divided in two.'

The inaugural champion, farmer's son Tom Shufflebotham, charmed 511 worms out of his plot in the allotted time of thirty minutes, and this record stood until 2009 when ten-year-old local girl Sophie Smith charmed an incredible 567 worms from her plot. Fierce local pride ensured that the trophy never left Willaston until 1996 when Wiltshire father-and-son team Phil and David Williams emerged victorious. However, it subsequently emerged that they had lived in Willaston for a number of years before moving south, so they were duly forgiven. The first tie-break occurred in 2003 when two teams both raised 167 worms from the ground. A further five-minute Charm Off was held in accordance with Rule 17, at the end of which Richard and Rodney Windsor defeated their rivals by just one worm.

While some eccentric British pursuits (such as the **World Walking the Plank Championships** on the Isle of Sheppey) have had to be scrapped in recent years because of health and safety concerns, worm charming has survived intact. However, it did come under attack some years ago from the New Zealand flat worm, which arrived in the area and threatened to do to the humble earthworm what the grey squirrel has done to the red. To ensure that there is no dearth of 'proper' worms for the June championships, each year a team of volunteers patrols the site of the Worm Arena for at least eight weeks beforehand in search of the evil interloper. They literally leave no stone unturned.

Inevitably, the competitive nature of the sport brings out the worst in some people. Participants have been known to chop worms in half in a bid to double their totals, and one man was banned for life after arriving on the school field with a supply of worms secreted down his trousers. Mike Forster said: 'We became suspicious when we saw he was wearing cycle clips. We became even more suspicious when we realised he had come by car.'

CHAPTER FOUR

TAKING IT TO EXTREMES

DEATHMATCH WRESTLING, JAPAN

The most common criticisms of the wrestling bouts that used to be shown on Saturday afternoon television were that they were too tame and nobody actually got hurt. The only people who seemed to believe the action was genuine were *World of Sport* commentator Kent Walton and the obligatory gaggle of handbag-wielding old ladies sitting in the front row of the audience who would defy their aged frailty by leaping to their feet and raining verbal and physical abuse on the bad guy whenever he was thrown out of the ring. Forget Lourdes: the fastest known cure for crippling arthritis and rheumatism was to have Mick McManus or Jackie Pallo land in your lap. However, nobody could ever accuse Japan's deathmatch wrestling contests of being too mild. These are exercises in savagery where, instead of using just their bare hands, fighters batter each other with an array of potentially lethal weapons, including axes, hammers, golf clubs, fluorescent light tubes, swords, fire extinguishers, steel chairs, and baseball bats covered in barbed wire. As an added twist, barbed wire is sometimes wrapped around the ring ropes or used to replace the ropes altogether. Fans have been known to ask for their money back if they haven't seen enough blood.

One of the leading promoters of deathmatch wrestling in Japan is Big Japan Pro Wrestling (BJW), which was formed in 1995 by former wrestlers Shinya Kojika and Kendo Nagasaki. Aware that the business is all about putting on a spectacular show to satisfy the punters' blood lust, BJW have devised a number of outrageous gimmick contests. Among these are:

- Steel cage deathmatches, where wrestlers pummel each other with weapons ranging from tables to crowbars in an arena with electrified walls.
- Ancient way deathmatches, where both fighters wrap their hands in hemp rope, which is then coated in sticky honey and dipped in broken glass.
- Circus deathmatches, where a scaffold is erected above the ring and beneath that scaffold is a 'safety net' made of barbed wire. When a wrestler has fallen off the scaffold and landed in the barbed wire, the net is cut away and the match continues to a pinfall, where the wrestler successfully pins the opponent's shoulders to the mat for a count of three.
- Razor deathmatches, where boards in the corners of the ring are fitted with razor blades.
- Piranha deathmatches, where barbed wire boards are placed in the corners and a tank full of live piranhas is set up in the centre of the ring. To win, you must hold your opponent in the tank for ten seconds.
- Scorpion deathmatches, which are similar to the piranha bouts, but instead of barbed wire boards, there are two large cacti in the corners, and instead of deadly fish, there is a tank of venomous scorpions. Note: poisonous snakes may be used if scorpions are not available.
- Crocodile deathmatches, where the loser of a deathmatch must then go on to wrestle a crocodile. This has only ever

been staged once, presumably because of the problems associated with fitting a pair of wrestling shorts on a crocodile.

To ramp up the thrill factor, the ring ropes are sometimes set on fire or fitted with small explosives. If nothing else, such measures would have deterred those belligerent old ladies from trying to climb into the ring.

Although nobody actually dies in these bouts, the blood is all too real, and the faces of seasoned deathmatch wrestlers such as Jun Kasai or Ryuji Ito suffer more cuts than the NHS. It should come as no surprise, therefore, to learn that the average deathmatch wrestler's career lasts around a third as long as that of a standard wrestler. But at least they can tell their grandchildren what it's like to be whacked in the face with a cactus wrapped in barbed wire. Not many people can say that.

EXTREME IRONING

For the uninitiated, extreme ironing (or EI) is a recently intro-duced sport in which daredevils take ironing boards to remote and challenging locations, where they proceed to iron items of clothing. It is said to combine the thrills of an extreme outdoor activity with the satisfaction of a well-pressed shirt.

The sport was conceived in Leicester in 1997 by Phil Shaw (or 'Steam' as he is known in EI circles) who, fancying an evening out rock climbing but faced with a mountain of ironing, decided to combine the two. As the sport caught on, fellow enthusiasts started ironing across gorges, underwater, on the ends of bungee ropes, while hanging upside down on the face of a climbing wall, on the back of a cow, and even while skydiving.

The first Extreme Ironing World Championships were held in a village near Munich in September 2002 and featured seventy competitors from ten countries, including Britain (who supplied three teams), Croatia, Australia, Austria, Chile and the host nation. Competitors were tested on their ability to cope with different fabrics in five challenging environments – water, where competi-tors used surfboards, canoes or rubber rings to help them iron on a fast-flowing Bavarian river; urban, which involved ironing in, on or around a broken car; forest, where competitors had to iron at the top of a tree; rocky, where they had to climb a purpose-built wall and iron a T-shirt; and freestyle, where ironing duties were performed in a location of the competitor's choice. Entrants were judged on their creative ironing skills as well as on the creases in the clothing. Of the 120 points on offer, the quality of the pressing counted for 60, style counted for 40, and speed 20. In his book *Extreme Ironing*, the definitive work on the subject, Shaw lamented: 'Ironists are sometimes so absorbed in getting themselves into some sort of awkward or dangerous situation with their ironing board that they forget the main reason they are there in the first place: to rid their clothes of creases and wrinkles.' After training for the event on Ben Nevis, Snowdon and other mountain settings, the British teams took gold and bronze in the team events while German and Austrian ironists carried off the individual prizes. These ranged from a holiday in Hawaii to the more coveted household goods.

Although the world championships have yet to be repeated, the sport has certainly not run out of steam. In 2003, Gloucestershire antiques dealer John Roberts and heating system designer Ben Gibbons flattened the altitude world record when they steamed up Mount Everest carrying an ironing board and ironed a Union Jack flag at 17,800 feet. They trekked for seventeen days to get to base camp with the board strapped to Gibbons' back and with Roberts carrying the iron. Clearly they had nothing more pressing to do. 'We ironed in some brilliant locations,' Roberts told the *Guardian*. 'We'd run out on to a 200-foot rope bridge and get the board out. People didn't know what to make of us. The Nepalese are great fun and understand the British sense of humour. They would join in with the ironing, whereas some of the Europeans thought we were deranged ... My mum's proud, but I don't think she's sure what she's proud of.'

The following year, Phil Shaw and two accomplices introduced extreme ironing to the United States because 'from a British person's point of view, you've never made it unless you've made it in America'. They ironed while kayaking in the sea, while climbing a quarry, and while hanging off the side of an old military amphibious vehicle. Shaw then endured eleven years of painful abstention to help his wife 'Starch' raise their family before returning to his beloved sport in 2015. There are now over 1,500 ironists worldwide. 'Our aim is to have the level of recognition that it becomes an Olympic sport,' Shaw told the *New York Times*. 'If you can have synchronised swimming and curling, I think extreme ironing has as much to offer.'

PALIO, SIENA, ITALY

When it comes to horses in sport, the Palio is about as far removed from the sedate elegance of dressage as is equinely possible. Held twice a year on 2 July and 16 August, Italy's most famous horse race is also its most dangerous and ruthless as jockeys ride horses bareback at breakneck speed around Siena's Piazzo del Campo in a modern-day equivalent of Ben Hur – but without the chariots.

The race dates back to 1656 and has remained largely unchanged ever since. Ten horses, representing ten of the seventeen districts (or *contrade*) of Siena, hurtle around three laps of the fan-shaped town square – a distance of about 1,100 metres. The Piazza simply isn't big enough for all seventeen to gallop around, but even with only ten there is carnage aplenty. The field is made up of the seven *contrade* that did not participate in the previous year's race and another three drawn by lots. Each *contrada* picks its jockey, but the respective horses are drawn by lots. A thick layer of dirt and turf is laid on the Piazza beforehand to provide a better surface, and although the race takes just ninety seconds, the preliminaries last much longer. Each horse is taken to the church of the district it is representing in order to be blessed before the altar. And the pre-race procession goes on for two hours because the Italians do love a spectacle. For the race itself, 30,000 spectators cram together in the centre of the square to watch the horses thunder past, while thousands more hang precariously from surrounding roofs, windows and balconies.

Padded barriers are erected to protect the animals at the tight corners, notably from the walls at the narrow San Martino curve where falls are commonplace, but despite these precautions fatalities do occur, with more than fifty horses reportedly being killed since 1970. It is tough on the jockeys too, as witnessed by the fact that the rules of the Palio state that the first horse to cross the line is the winner, with or without a rider. Jockeys are allowed to use their whips, not only on their own horses but also for hindering other horses and riders. They can also pull and shove each other and deliberately block opposing horses at the start. The only thing considered illegal is grabbing the reins of another horse. All in all, it's not exactly the sort of behaviour you would expect to see at Royal Ascot. The rivalry between the seventeen *contrade* is so fierce that supporters take almost as much delight in their bitterest enemy losing as they do in victory. At the July 2015 race, jockey Giovanni Atzeni, riding for Nicchio, the district of the Shell, had barely rounded the first bend when he was dragged from his horse by the jockey representing Shell's rival district, Valdimontone, the Ram. The Valdimontone jockey sacrificed all hope of victory by his actions but, in unseating his rival, his hero status in the district was assured. In the circumstances it is scarcely a surprise that bribery is routine, doping is not exactly unheard of, and the day sometimes ends in outbreaks of violence among followers. No wonder the *New York Times* labelled a 2015 documentary film of the spectacle as '*Rocky* on horseback'.

The most successful Palio jockey of all time is Andrea Degortes, nicknamed *Aceto* ('Vinegar'), who registered fourteen wins between 1964 and 1996. The leading current rider is Luigi Bruschelli with twelve wins, although he claims he has thirteen because his horse won without him one year. In the 2015 film *Palio*, Bruschelli describes the typical tactics of the Palio rider: 'Once you know how good your horse is then you decide what to aim for, either to block your enemy or go for the win.' It is very much a case of win or bust; nobody wants to know a brave runner-up. Indeed, in the Palio, the loser is traditionally not the one who comes last; it is the one who finishes second.

SEPAK BOLA API, INDONESIA

To welcome the Muslim holy month of Ramadan, students in parts of Indonesia play a game of football called sepak bola api. Two teams of eleven players kick a ball and try to shoot it into the opposing goal. Nothing unusual in that you may think . . . except that the ball is on fire and they play barefoot. In sepak bola api, every player is a hotshot.

The players' preparation for the game is all-important. There are no pre-match steaks or energy drinks – instead they pray a lot and fast for twenty-one days beforehand, only eating when the sun goes down and even then scrupulously avoiding all foods cooked with fire. This is supposed to make them immune to the flames and enable them to kick and handle the fireball without getting burned. Just in case it doesn't work, they first soak their feet in a non-flammable mixture of herbs and spices. Try selling this line to Cristiano Ronaldo or Lionel Messi.

Since a regular football would quickly melt if set ablaze, the game is played with a special ball made from a coconut shell. The outer skin and the milk inside the coconut are removed, the shell is punctured with the tip of a knife, and the ball is then soaked in petrol or kerosene for up to seven days to ensure that it will remain alight throughout the match. It is the only game of soccer where too much dribbling might put the ball out. The pitch is bare and rough, and as you might imagine, headers in sepak bola api (which means 'flaming football') are comparatively rare. Quite apart from the risk of singed hair, not many are too keen on heading a coconut. Quick feet are essential and blistering pace is an occasional side effect rather than an asset, but incredibly, the players almost always emerge from their Ramadan-a-ding-dong unscathed even though their feet and legs are left covered in black ash. Playing with a ball that is constantly on fire also reduces the need for floodlights. Nevertheless, one suspects there might be a few complaints if FIFA decide to use a burning coconut at the next World Cup.

SKACH KOYL, TODOS SANTOS, GUATEMALA

On 1 November each year, a bizarre horse race takes place in Guatemala, in which horses are ridden back and forth along a 100-metre-long rough dirt track in the mountain village of Todos Santos for seven hours. Oh, and one other thing: all the riders are drunk!

Skach Koyl ('The Race of Souls') is an old Mayan custom run to mark the country's annual Day of the Dead celebrations. In the seventeenth century, the Spanish invaders, having conquered the local Mayans, promptly banned them from riding horses. So the practice of drunk horse riding began as a symbol of rebellion, and continues to this day as a protest against colonialism and as a way of paying respect to the dead. The big race preparations start the day before, when a chicken is sacrificed to bless the track. All riders must abstain from sex that night, which is probably just as well because instead they spend the hours of darkness getting hopelessly drunk, often on a local brew called Quetzalteca. Since tradition dictates that they hardly drink for the rest of the year, this sudden binge goes straight to their heads and by noon on race day, men and boys as young as twelve can be seen slumped in corners or lying in ditches around the village. It is reminiscent of just about any British town or city on a Friday night. It is with jockeys in this advanced state of intoxication that the race gets under way. They look the part – dressed in Mayan costume of red and white pants, purple shirts and straw hats – but a handful are incapable of climbing on to a horse, so require a little assistance. Some are so drunk they have to be strapped into the saddle to prevent them falling off as soon as the horse moves. Steering can also be a mite wayward, especially when the riders decide to showboat by letting go of the reins altogether and careering along the track hands-free.

As you might expect from such a haphazard concept, there are no real rules and no start or finish as such. In the course of the seven hours, riders stop whenever they please, either to take on more alcohol or to sleep it off under a hedge for half an hour. The more dedicated jockeys and drinkers actually ride while clutching a can of beer. Naturally those who can hold their liquor fare best, not least because they are more likely to remain on top of their horse for longer. Generally in horse racing this is considered a good thing. Accidents are commonplace and are sometimes serious, but even if a rider has the misfortune to be killed, all is not lost because, according to local tradition, a dead jockey is considered an offering to the underworld that will produce fertile crops the following year. So that's okay, then.

The winning rider, who is judged on bravery and endurance, is rewarded with the prize of a live chicken and the title of 'El Capitan'. Mayan tradition dictates that menfolk take part in Skach Koyl four times in their life. It is considered a rite of passage, and in their final year, they triumphantly carry live chickens as they ride. You have to feel for the chicken.

Once upon a time, as many as a hundred riders took part in the annual stampede, but recently the field has dwindled to around twenty. One who was probably relieved by the decline was the local mayor, Modesto Mendez, who in 2009 tried to ban the sale of hard alcohol in the village following a spate of nasty falls in the race. 'People here aren't able to hold their drink,' he explained to Reuters. 'If they have one drink, they just continue until they're so drunk they want to hit someone.' His pleas fell on deaf ears. At that year's race there were a number of falls, one rider was carried away by bystanders after being trampled underfoot, and there were reports of drunken spectators stumbling through the village. It seems that some traditions are simply too good to lose.

VOLCANO BOARDING, CERRO NEGRO, NICARAGUA

If your idea of an extreme sport is crazy golf, then volcano boarding – or volcano surfing as it is sometimes called – may not necessarily be for you. For it involves riding a piece of wood down an active volcano at speeds of up to 50mph.

The most popular venue for volcano boarding is the 2,388-foot-high Cerro Negro in Nicaragua, possibly because it has not erupted since 1999. However, that was its twentieth eruption, and since the volcano was only formed in 1850, that works out at an eruption every eight years or so. Just in case things do look like getting a bit lively again, its activity is monitored regularly for the safety of the boarders. It takes forty-five minutes to hike to the top of Cerro Negro but only three minutes to hurtle back down on a wooden board. This can either be done standing up, as on a snowboard, or sitting down as you would on a sledge. Although the former may look more impressive, those who have tried say it is more restrictive because turning is difficult and it is also considerably slower. There is also a greater chance of falling off – the slope is forty-one degrees at its steepest – and crashing into sharp volcanic rock, which is why riders are given protective jump suits, goggles, knee-pads and sturdy leather gloves. Unfortunately the orange suits make them look more like a gang of convicts than sporty thrill seekers. The volcano boards have a rope at the front, which sitting riders grip while simultaneously leaning back to achieve maximum speed. The underside of the sledge is covered with a thin layer of metal, and glued to this is a strip of plastic to reduce friction and create extra speed. The plastic has to be replaced every day because it burns off after only a couple of runs. This gives an indication of what rough volcanic ash will do to your flesh and why it is therefore not a wise move to fall off at any point during the descent.

The man who saw the potential for boarding down Cerro Negro was Australian tour guide, Darryn Webb. He was a keen practitioner of the sport of sandboarding in Queensland, but once he visited the volcano around 2004 he realised that it could make a great boarding venue. For here was a dune-like slope, only bigger and blacker, and with the added thrill of possible eruption. Webb's first descent was on that most unlikely of vehicles, a mini-bar fridge. Next he tried a mattress and then a door. Eventually he concluded that, for mass participation, a modified sledge would be more practical.

If Cerro Negro doesn't sound dramatic enough, volcano boarding also takes place occasionally on the 1,184-foot slopes of Mount Yasur on Tanna, an island of Vanuatu in the Pacific. The difference here is that the volcano erupts on a daily basis, meaning that there is a high risk of breathing in poisonous gases and your adrenalin rush could be hotly pursued by a rush of molten lava. Journalist Zoltan Istvan, one of the few who has tried it, described 'lava bombs the size of Rottweilers flying over my head and on to the slope below me', and likened the whole experience to Russian roulette.

For now though, most volcano boarders visit Nicaragua and give thanks to the intrepid Australian who first looked up at the charcoal slopes and thought: 'I wonder if I could ride my fridge down that?'

WORLD SAUNA CHAMPIONSHIPS, HEINOLA,
FINLAND (DISCONTINUED)

Held annually in Heinola, Finland, the World Sauna Championships were an extreme endurance contest to find the competitor who could remain in a hot, sweltering sauna the longest. One described it as 'a battle to see whose skin boils last'. Dressed in swimsuits, the participants had to sit with their buttocks and thighs on the bench, elbows on their knees, and arms folded. If they touched any part of their skin other than wiping sweat from their face, they were disqualified. The starting temperature inside was 110°C – already ten degrees above the boiling point of water – and every thirty seconds half a litre of water was thrown on to the stove to crank up the heat. The winner was the last person to stay in the sauna and be able to walk out without needing assistance. It was not a sport for the faint-hearted.

The rules of the contest stipulated that all body creams and lotions were to be removed beforehand and any long hair had to be tied up in a ponytail. Alcohol was strictly forbidden immediately prior to and during the competition. Sauna sitters were not allowed to disturb each other, and, at the request of the judges, had to show that they retained control of their senses in the intense heat by giving a thumbs-up. It was also not considered a good idea to slap the winner on the back afterwards by way of congratulations.

The championships were first held in 1999 and, in a country of five million people and nearly two million saunas, they quickly became a nationally televised event. Finns sit in saunas with the same enthusiasm that the British sit in pubs. Contestants from more than twenty countries took part, but nearly always struggled to match the endurance levels of the Finns. Many lasted only a minute or two, and even those with the toughest skin often gave up after six minutes, but in 2003 Finland's Timo Kaukonen somehow managed to stay in the sauna for a world record 16 minutes 15 seconds. Kaukonen went on to win the title on four more occasions but then in 2010 the event reached a tragic climax. Kaukonen himself and Russia's Vladimir Ladyzhensky passed out after spending six minutes in the sauna, both suffering from terrible burns. Ladyzhensky died from his injuries and Kaukonen was rushed to hospital, where thankfully he eventually recovered. As both were automatically disqualified for not leaving the sauna unaided, Ilkka Pöyhiä was declared the winner.

In the aftermath of the tragedy, the World Sauna Championships were suspended indefinitely. The following year, the City of Heinola confirmed that it would no longer be hosting the event because it felt that competitive sauna sitting had lost its 'original playful and joyous characteristics'. When competitors talk of 'swallowing each breath like a gulp of scorching soup', 'triceps riddled with pebble-sized blisters' and 'ears split open and bubbling', it is hard to imagine how it was ever considered playful and joyous.

CHAPTER FIVE

TARGET PRACTICE

TEJO, COLOMBIA

Have you ever stopped to think how much more dramatically unpredictable a game of darts would be if the board were packed with explosives? Imagine the TV viewing figures if Phil 'The Power' Taylor risked losing a finger or two whenever he went for a treble twenty. Like darts, the Colombian national sport of tejo involves hurling a steel projectile at a target and is invariably played against a backdrop of wholesale beer consumption, but it has the added ingredient of gunpowder. This is exploding darts, or lawn bowls with land mines.

Tejo is based on a game invented by indigenous warriors over four hundred and fifty years ago, and was often played to earn the right to wed a maiden from a rival tribe. Poker – or, perhaps in more distinguished communities, Scrabble – would later go on to fulfil a similar function in winning the hand of a beloved. Nothing says 'I love you' more than a triple-word score with a double-letter score on the 'X'. Tejo gameplay consisted of throwing golden discs into a distant hole. The gold-hungry Spanish conquistadors wasted little time in melting down the discs to add to their personal wealth but they did refine the game – if refine is quite the word – by adding explosives to the mix.

Today, the game requires competitors to lob 680-gram steel pucks – called tejos – underhand into a one-metre-square clay-filled box that is located at the far end of the playing lane some twenty metres away. The box is tilted towards the throwers at an angle of about forty degrees. Up to four small paper triangles packed with gunpowder, called 'mechas', rest on the lip of a metal circle – or 'bocin' – in the centre of the box. Players score one point for getting closer to the circle than their opponents, three points for lighting the gunpowder on impact, six points for getting their puck in the circle, and a maximum nine points for achieving all three. The first player or team to reach twenty-seven points is the winner. A protective board at the back of the box is designed to prevent the heavy tejos from hitting innocent bystanders. The potential flashpoint does not necessarily occur with the throwing of the tejos; it is when the players attempt to retrieve them from the clay box – the equivalent of removing thrown darts from the board – that they have to be on their guard. That is when the slightest contact can lead the gunpowder in the mecha to explode without warning, and it explains why many veteran tejo players are missing the odd eye or finger.

Although tejo is primarily played by adults, Colombian youngsters take part in special youth leagues, because what could possibly go wrong when you put children near explosives? Among the more safety-conscious, there have been moves to introduce technotejo, in which the gunpowder-filled mechas are replaced by electronic sensors. In the meantime, traditionalists prefer to carry on playing a game where it's not only the beer-fuelled players that have short fuses.

WORLD BLACK PUDDING THROWING CHAMPIONSHIPS, RAMSBOTTOM, LANCASHIRE, ENGLAND

The story behind one of Britain's quirkiest sporting events varies depending on who you ask. Some say that back in 1455 at the height of the Wars of the Roses between the Houses of Lancaster and York, the warring factions met at the little-known Battle of Stubbins Bridge in Lancashire, and when the armies ran out of ammunition, they started throwing local food delicacies at each other – black puddings from the Lancastrians and Yorkshire puddings from the Yorkists. However, this theory has been resoundingly debunked by noted historian Lucy Worsley, so is probably nothing more than a colourful legend. Others claim that in the nineteenth century, Yorkshire folk bound for a seaside holiday in Blackpool used to stop off at the Corner Pin public house at Stubbins for refreshment. They would feel so refreshed that they started fighting the locals. One day, the inn's landlord, a man named Higginbottom, saw a group of youngsters throwing stones at the Yorkshire puddings that had been left to cool down on the ledges of the pub roof prior to lunch. Obviously being of an entrepreneurial nature, he decided to turn it into a mini War of the Roses between Yorkshire and Lancashire, with black puddings replacing stones. Again, it's a good story, but there is no evidence to suggest that there is any more truth in this version of events than in the historical food fight.

What does seem certain is that the contest originated at the Corner Pin in the 1830s before falling from grace and then being revived in the 1980s. It has now acquired the title of the World Black Pudding Throwing Championships (formerly the World Black Pudding Knocking Championships) and is held on the second Sunday in September, each year attracting hundreds of entrants from all corners of the globe, including the United States, Australia, New Zealand, Canada, Hong Kong, Kenya, Peru and Argentina. The sport acquired unlikely kudos with an unofficial demonstration at the 2002 Commonwealth Games in Manchester. Since the Corner Pin closed, the venue has switched to the Royal Oak pub in nearby Ramsbottom, and the event starts at 11 a.m. and ends at 4 p.m. Instead of being placed on a pub roof, the six-and-half-pound Yorkshire puddings are now arranged in a pile of twelve on a twenty-foot-high plinth. Competitors wielding six-ounce black puddings stand on the ground on a purpose-built golden grid called the oche and aim three underarm lobs up at the pile of Yorkshires, hoping to knock down as many as possible. Each black pudding projectile is wrapped in a pair of women's tights. This is to prevent it falling apart in flight rather than to enhance the taste. A ladder is in constant use to replace fallen Yorkshire puddings. These must be of solid consistency, which can mean changing them regularly if the event takes place in wet weather. For as any black pudding thrower will tell you, a soggy Yorkshire is more difficult to displace than a crispy one. The first prize used to be the winner's height in beer but is now £100.

Hurling cooked pig's blood through the air is an art in itself according to the organisers, and throwers have devised all sorts of spins and trajectories to achieve maximum devastation of Yorkshires. 'It's skilful,' said one. 'You can't throw overarm – you've got to throw underarm and it's got to be precise, otherwise you won't hit any puddings. You try lobbing a pudding under-hand twenty foot up – you've got to have some weight behind you to do that.' This was underlined by the 2015 winner, Mark Swinton, who managed to dislodge an impressive eight Yorkshire puddings from the plinth with his three throws. 'I'm a hod carrier by trade,' he told the *Manchester Evening News*, 'so I have a very strong right arm.' The message is clear: when it comes to black pudding throwing, weaklings need not apply.

WORLD CUSTARD PIE CHAMPIONSHIPS,
COXHEATH, KENT, ENGLAND

As you might expect from a sporting competition featuring that clown's staple the custard pie, there is nothing subtle about the World Custard Pie Championships that take place each year in Kent in early June. But just as slapstick is invariably more fun to perform than it is to watch, so the competitors enjoy every minute, even if they are on the receiving end.

Two teams of four people wearing fancy dress stand next to a table and throw the pies at their opponents who are standing eight feet away. A direct hit in the face earns six points, a hit on the chest three points, and a hit on any other part of the body brings one point. A player who misses three times in a row has one point deducted. According to the official rules, every player must throw left-handed, so a sensible tip would be to pack your team with people who are naturally left-handed. There is no obligation to remain motionless while your opponents line up their shots, but you must stay roughly in position. Hiding behind your team table is definitely not in the spirit of the occasion and will incur the wrath of the judges. Around thirty teams take part and each pie fight lasts between fifteen and thirty seconds.

Said to have been inspired by Charlie Chaplin, the championships were created by a former Mayor of Maidstone, Mike FitzGerald, and were first held in 1967 as a way of raising funds for Coxheath village hall. Over the years, they have attracted the cream of international competition from such far-flung lands as Canada, Finland and Germany. However, pride of place must go to the Japanese team who travelled halfway around the world in 2015 for the sole purpose of throwing custard pies at total strangers. 'We came all the way from Japan just to win this competition,' they said after a day of hard training. 'So we will win.' And they did. They even returned to defend their title in 2016, only to be beaten in the semi-final.

In the early years, it was a male-only event, but eventually women were also allowed to take part. Slowly these bastions were being broken down. First the vote, then the World Custard Pie Championships.

With echoes of the World Cup in 1966, the custard pie trophy went missing in 1987 and, with no Pickles on hand to retrieve it, the valued silverware was never found. As a result, the event lost some of its lustre and was discontinued for a while before being resurrected in 2007. As befits such an iconic contest, the recipe for the pies remains a closely guarded secret, but rumour has it that they contain little more than flour and water. More than two thousand pies are flung in mock anger each year. The competitors may not need to be fortified by drink beforehand, but it is the one event where most of them leave pie-eyed.

WORLD EGG THROWING CHAMPIONSHIPS,
SWATON, LINCOLNSHIRE, ENGLAND

No one likes to be left with egg on their face, but at the World Egg Throwing Championships in Lincolnshire it is an even more important consideration than usual. For the coveted title of world champion goes to the pair who can throw and catch their egg over the greatest distance without the shell breaking.

The World Egg Throwing Federation, formed in 2004, states that egg throwing has been a sport enjoyed by millions of people 'since early humans discovered the delight of watching a failure of another to catch a tossed egg'. The organised sport of egg throwing is thought to date back to at least 1322, when the newly appointed Abbot of Swaton took possession of the parish by royal decree. As the only person in the area to own chickens, he apparently decided to bribe the peasants to attend church by promising each attendee an egg. However, when the local river flooded, preventing people getting to church, the monks would hurl the eggs over the water to the waiting peasants. It is also said that in times of severe flooding, they used small trebuchets to obtain the extra distance required. It is from these humble beginnings that the sport of egg throwing developed and it has been played ever since in the village, especially at fetes and fairs. WETF president Andy Dunlop told the BBC: 'People see it as not a real sport, but it is. There are people travelling across the world for these things. It pre-dates everything like football and rugby – lesser sports – and cricket even. Top athletes take part in the throw and catch, which is far more skilful than the javelin, because no one bothers to catch that.'

The world championships were first held in 2006 and take place on the last Sunday in June. The two team members start standing ten metres apart, the distance between them being increased after each successful throw and catch. The team members alternate throwing and catching responsibilities, and the catcher, who is not allowed to wear gloves or carry a net, must not move from his starting position until the egg is airborne. The first winners were New Zealand turkey farmers Andrew McKay and Nigel Tiffin, who claimed that they had been practising for the event for twenty years at home using emu eggs. Some weeks later, the disbelieving mother of one of the duo contacted the WETF to ask if her son's unlikely story about being a world champion was true. She was profoundly shocked to be informed that it was. In 2014, local pair 'Ginge' Harrison and 'Titch' Wells won for the second year running with a successful throw of fifty metres, smashing competition from Ireland, Germany and the United States.

Another event on the same bill is the **World Russian Egg Roulette Championship**, a test of nerve where competitors strive to avoid smashing a raw egg on their head. For each knockout contest, two competitors wearing head bandanas for protection sit opposite one another at a table. On the table is a box containing five hard-boiled eggs and one raw egg. Using either judgement based on years of experience or just guessing, players take it in turns to select an egg and then smash it on to their forehead. The one who finds the raw egg loses the match and his or her dignity.

WORLD PEA SHOOTING CHAMPIONSHIPS, WITCHAM, CAMBRIDGESHIRE, ENGLAND

When John Tyson, headmaster of the village school at Witcham, caught some mischievous pupils amusing themselves by pinging their unfortunate schoolmates with dried peas, he not only confiscated the weapons but had the idea of staging a pea-shooting competition to raise funds for the village hall. The gesture might not have gone down well with all of his young students, but it proved so popular with the rest of the community that the World Pea Shooting Championships have been staged in Witcham every summer since 1971. They currently take place on the second Saturday in July. In memory of his contribution to the world of sport, the name of every pea-shooting champion is inscribed on the John Tyson Shield.

The target at the world championships measures one foot in diameter and is surfaced with putty so that the peas stick in place upon impact. There are three circles: the inner circle scores five points, the middle circle three points, and the outer circle one point. Peas must be fired at the target from a distance of twelve feet by blowing with the mouth. No other orifice is permitted. The shooters can be made of any material but must not exceed twelve inches in length. Only peas provided by the organisers may be used. The competition is run on a knockout basis, with each person firing five peas alternately. In the finals, competitors fire a total of ten peas alternately. In the separate team event, each player shoots five peas consecutively. This allows some to put all five peas in the mouth at the same time and then, by deft use of the tongue, fire them off in machine-gun fashion. This is considered elite pea shooting.

Although the event has been dominated by local people, there has occasionally been an international flavour, notably in the form of American personnel from the nearby US airbases of RAF Mildenhall and RAF Lakenheath. Beginner's luck can prevail – when Emma Watson (no relation to the actress) became ladies' world champion in 2011, it was the first time she had ever picked up a peashooter – but generally it is the seasoned pros who come out on top. In 2016, Jim Collins won his third Open title and Michelle Berry retained the ladies' title for the third year in a row, using a laser shooter made by her father. For don't be fooled into thinking that nobody takes pea shooting seriously. In order to improve their aim, competitors have been known to employ expensive telescopic rifle sights. Some people will go to any lengths to become a world champion.

CHAPTER SIX

FEATS OF STRENGTH

BOKDROL SPOEG, SOUTH AFRICA

No doubt kudu dung has many practical uses – converted into a fuel or dried as a nice ornament, perhaps – but it is hard to imagine why anyone thought of making a sport out of spitting it. Yet kudu dung spitting – or bokdrol spoek/spoeg – is so popular among the Afrikaner community in South Africa that it has its own national competition.

Official events use either kudu or impala dung pellets – only true dung-spitting aficionados can taste the difference – but other breeds of antelope are available. The competitor begins by dropping the pellet into a shot glass filled with alcohol in order to sterilise it, then downs the liquor, catches the pellet in his teeth and spits it as far as possible. The spit can be made from a stationary position or with a run-up, the distance being measured according to where the dung finally comes to rest rather than where it first hits the ground. Experts say the secret is to find a nice hard pellet and not to let it melt on your tongue, should you ever be tempted to confuse it with a Malteser. In 2006, Shaun van Rensburg reportedly spat a lump of kudu dung a world-record distance of fifty-one feet.

The origins of kudu dung spitting can be traced back to the frustration of early hunters. The animals were usually too quick for them, with the result that by the time the hunters arrived on the scene hoping to make a kill, all they were left with was a cloud of dust and a pile of poop. They cursed their luck by picking up the poop and then spitting it in the direction of their departing meal. Over time, this developed into a local custom, which in turn became competitive. In 1994, it was recognised as a formal sport.

Even the most seasoned spitters are reluctant to put fresh dung into their mouth. Instead they prefer to let it dry in the sun until it becomes firm and loses a little of its natural flavour. After all, there are usually plenty of pellets to choose from. Also, a firm poop flies further, and that's what bokdrol spoeg is all about. Consequently, constipated kudus are much sought-after. The sport is now used widely as an initiation ceremony for overseas tourists, to give them a taste of South Africa, so to speak. The key is to have a guide who can tell one type of dung from another so that you don't end up with zebra or wildebeest poop in your mouth. Clearly that would never do.

FRUITCAKE TOSS, MANITOU SPRINGS, COLORADO, USA

Observing that friends never seemed to want to eat the fruitcakes they had received as Christmas gifts, Michele Carvell, former Chamber of Commerce Director for Manitou Springs, Colorado, came up with a wizard wheeze for disposing of the unwanted foodstuff – a sporting contest. Thus in 1996 was born the Great Fruitcake Toss, an event which, in its heyday, attracted up to a thousand competitors every January.

The world record was set at the 2013 event when Joe Jeanjaquet completed a hat-trick of victories by tossing his fruitcake a distance of 415 feet at the local high school playing field. There is no subtle way of putting this, but Jeanjaquet is a hand tosser; he propels his cake by hand. However, a separate arm of the contest was opened to mechanical devices, some of which would not have looked out of place at NASA. They were capable of launching fruitcakes far and wide to distances beyond measurement. In 2013, one official distance was recorded as 'destination unknown'. While these rocket launchers and giant catapults may have enhanced the fruitcake-tossing spectacle, they also contributed to the event being temporarily cancelled in 2014. Leslie Lewis of the Manitou Springs Chamber of Commerce explained to the *Colorado Springs Gazette*: 'These more powerful fruitcake launchers had begun to send cakes into residential areas. When you hit businesses and houses it's not a good thing.'

When the contest returned in 2015, the venue switched to a local park, and the mechanical devices were absent. It was back to good old-fashioned tossing. The distance event (measured to where the cake stops rolling as opposed to where it lands) remains the most popular, but there are also competitions to test accuracy – a bit like archery with two-pound fruitcakes instead of arrows.

Most accept that the greatest distance is to be achieved by throwing the cake overarm like a javelin, but a few try to emulate the style of the discus while others prefer an ungainly underarm hurl. All brought-in fruitcakes are inspected beforehand to ensure that they do not contain any substance so hard that a wayward throw could injure onlookers. Imagine having to fill in an insurance form to report that you had been hit by a flying fruitcake.

Joe Jeanjaquet and his wife Hillary, a two-time champion in her own right, have been known to use cakes that had been stored in the freezer for six long years. In the world of fruitcake tossing, the keywords are fruit, nuts, flour and preparation. Even if you don't own unwanted confectionery that you wish to send into orbit, you can rent a fruitcake on the day for a dollar. As we have seen from the Emma Crawford Coffin Races, there is no shortage of fruitcakes in Manitou Springs.

INTERNATIONAL CHERRY PIT SPITTING
CHAMPIONSHIP, EAU CLAIRE, MICHIGAN, USA

Football had the Charltons, cricket had the Chappells, and Formula One had the Hills, but when it comes to world-class cherry pit spitting, the Krause family have always been the ones to beat. Rick 'Pellet Gun' Krause is a multiple champion and when the years of spitting cherry stones finally started to take their toll, his son Brian 'Young Gun' Krause took it to a new level with a spit of 93 foot 6.5 inches at the 2004 International Cherry Pit Spitting Championship. Later that day, and away from the strict rules that govern the sport, the twenty-six-year-old managed to spit a pit an astonishing distance of 110 foot 4 inches in the freestyle event, but it was not recognised as a true world record because he did not remain flat-footed when launching his spit.

Each contestant gets three tries and has one minute between spits to eat the fruit off the cherry. If a pit is accidentally swallowed, that spit is forfeited. No foreign objects that might give an advantage when spitting may be held in the mouth, but denture racks are provided for those wishing to remove their teeth. Hands must be kept below the shoulders to prevent the illegal practice of cheek popping. As height is considered an advantage in cherry pit spitting – except on windy days – taller competitors have to stand further back. After measuring the distance, the judges sensibly wear gloves to remove the ejected stones. Rick Krause has no doubt as to what makes a champion cherry pit spitter. 'You've got to be able to roll your tongue and make sure you get a really tight seal with the pit. It's all in the tongue.'

The championship, which is held in early July to coincide with the start of the cherry harvest, began in 1974 and Rick Krause made his mark in 1980 when he picked up his first title. Brian, then aged three, made his debut the following year. In the Krause family, first you learn how to walk, then you learn how to spit cherry pits. For the next three decades, the Krauses pretty much reigned supreme. At the 1996 event, Rick married Marlene, herself a thirty-foot-plus spitter whose competition nickname is 'Machine Gun'. Then, in 2012, first-time unknown Ronn Matt, a Chicago delivery driver, rocked the sport to its foundations by lifting the title. It was like a Shetland pony winning the Grand National. Brian Krause was heard to mutter: 'Every squirrel finds a nut once in a while.' In 2013, the natural order was restored, however, with a third Krause – Brian's younger brother Matt 'BB Gun' – claiming the crown. As he went up to accept the world championship belt and trophy for the first time, his father yelled: 'Now I can stop telling everyone you're adopted!' It can be tough being part of the world's most famous cherry pit spitting dynasty.

Incredibly, in 2016, at the ripe old age of sixty-two, Rick Krause exceeded all expectorations by spitting out a fourteen-footer to claim his sixteenth title, pushing son Brian into second place and beating him by more than a foot. With every American spitter worth his salt keen to topple the Krauses, interest in the event shows no sign of dropping away. Herb Teichman, the championship founder and owner of the venue, the Tree-Mendus Fruit Farm, told the Michigan Local Legacies website: 'Cherry pit spitting is a nutritious sport. It's the most entertaining way to dispose of the pit after you've eaten the cherry. The pit spit is a global demonstration that healthy eating, deep breathing and physical exercise can be accomplished simultaneously, in public, with only a minimal loss of dignity. Actually, cherry pit spitting is like a good sneeze. They're both therapeutic.'

KIRKPINAR OIL WRESTLING
CHAMPIONSHIPS, EDIRNE, TURKEY

If you have ever struggled to pick up a wet bar of soap that has fallen in the bath, you will get some idea of the problems facing competitors at the Kırkpınar Oil Wrestling Championships. Wearing a pair of leather trousers called a *kisbet* and with their upper bodies smeared in copious amounts of slippery olive oil, they grapple with each other in an event that was first staged as far back as 1360.

By then, oil wrestling had already been practised for centuries in the Middle East, the oil originally applied to soldiers' bodies as an insect repellent. Legend has it that in the fourteenth century, two Ottoman soldiers, bored and in need of entertainment while raiding forts on what is now Turkey's border with Greece and Bulgaria, began wrestling each other. The Sultan offered a pair of leather trousers to the winner, and both men were so keen to claim the prize that the fight continued right through the night. The exhausted combatants were found dead the next morning, their bodies still apparently intertwined. They were buried beneath a fig tree, after which their comrades hurried off to capture Edirne and make it the capital of the Ottoman Empire. When the troops reached another fig tree at nearby Kırkpınar Meadow, they staged a forty-man wrestling competition in honour of their two fallen friends, and the tournament has continued annually ever since.

Around a thousand wrestlers – or *pehlivan* – both boys and men, take part in the three-day competition in twelve categories that are ranked by height rather than weight. A fight is won when one wrestler manages to lift his opponent above his head or pins him to the floor. When pairs locked in combat break away from each other, they sometimes trade slaps to the head, aiming to make the opponent dizzy, disoriented and less able to fend off the next attack. Obviously it is not easy to grab a large man covered in oil, so many pull on the drawstrings of their opponent's trousers, which is a perfectly legal move. More worryingly, they can even grab inside the trousers, searching for leverage, although genital and rectal holds are forbidden. Just in case there are any violations, the olive oil used is probably extra virgin.

Bouts take place simultaneously on a huge grassy area, each contest having its own referee. Whereas they used to last for days, they are now limited to forty minutes, with an extra fifteen minutes if there is no winner in that time. The victor traditionally kisses his opponent at the end of the contest, which, if you've been rummaging around inside his trousers for the past half-hour, seems only reasonable. A box of chocolates wouldn't go amiss either. The overall champion – or chief pehlivan – is presented with a golden belt, which he gets to keep if he wins it three years in a row. The last man to do so was Ahmet Tasci in 1998. It is estimated that the organisers get through 100 drums of olive oil in the course of the championships, which take place in July, the hottest time of the year. The scent of sizzling bodies, nicely browning one side, fills the air.

Lest you think you can immediately perfect a half nelson just by throwing a bottle of cooking oil over yourself, most of these men have been trained in oil wrestling for years by a master of the art. The pehlivan are also supposed to uphold traditional Turkish values, such as generosity, honesty, respectfulness, and being crap at the Eurovision Song Contest.

MOBILE PHONE THROWING WORLD
CHAMPIONSHIPS, SAVONLINNA, FINLAND

From the land that pioneered the sports of wife carrying and sauna sitting comes another bizarre world championship – mobile phone throwing. Finland considers itself very much the home of mobile phone production, but acknowledges that for all their benefits, they can be frustrating devices, occasionally prompting their owners to feel the desire to hurl them a great distance. We're talking credit that runs out partway through an important call, suddenly finding that you have no connection to the outside world simply because your train has entered a tunnel, or when you discover that you've accidentally sent the selfie of your genitalia to your mother. 'This contest speaks to people the world over, as mobile phones are a blessing and a curse,' say the event organisers. 'Phones have become a part of the modern man, and sometimes many of us would like to remove that part. This is the only sport where you can pay back all the frustrations and disappointments caused by this modern equipment.'

The championships were actually devised as a novel and safe way of disposing of old mobile phones. Instead of recycling their phones, many users simply throw them out – insurance companies estimate that thousands of unwanted phones have been dumped in lakes across Finland. The batteries in the phones become a toxic waste, damaging the environment, so in 2000 a leading Finnish insurance company sponsored the first Mobile Phone Throwing World Championships in the south-eastern town of Savonlinna, about two hundred miles from Nokia HQ.

There are two main categories in competitive phone throwing – original and freestyle. In original, the winner is simply the person who throws their phone the greatest distance in a basic

167

overarm manner; in freestyle, marks are awarded for style, aesthetics and creative choreography. For example, Taco Cohen of the Netherlands, the winner of the men's freestyle event at the 2007 world championships, came up with a spectacular routine that combined juggling and acrobatics. He didn't even bother throwing his phone. Any phone weighing over 200 grams is eligible for either section, and these are provided by the organisers, which is disappointing for those competitors who have personal reasons for wanting to throw their own old phones as far away as possible. There is no dope testing, but the jury will bar any competitor whom they deem to be mentally or physically unfit to throw. The prize for becoming world champion is a new mobile phone.

The 2013 world championships attracted more than eighty competitors from six countries, although the Finns retained their grip on mobile phone throwing. The men's distance champion was Riku Haverinen with a throw of 320 feet, the length of a football pitch. The freestyle division was won by Erika Vilpponen, who threw the phone backwards over her shoulder while riding a circus bike, thus disposing of an old phone in a thoroughly *irresponsible* manner.

The success of the world championships has seen mobile phone throwing events crop up in various other countries, including the intermittently staged **UK Mobile Phone Throwing Championships** in London's Battersea Park. In 2009 and 2010, these were held alongside the **Sumo Suit Athletics World Championships**, where competitors performed regular track and field events while wearing sumo fat suits. The bar is set low at the high jump.

TUNA TOSS, PORT LINCOLN, SOUTH AUSTRALIA

The Australian coastal town of Port Lincoln is synonymous with tuna fishing. Back in the 1970s, when overflowing trawlers arrived back in port, men would stand on the decks of the boats and throw the tuna up on to waiting trucks. This was no mean feat because a hefty tuna can tip the scales at 400 pounds or more, so they naturally concentrated on the smaller fish. Even so, it was a job that required considerable muscle power. Times were tough economically, and young lads looking for a few hours' paid work used to line up along the quayside hoping to cash in when the tuna boats returned. To be taken on, they had to pass a simple test. This did not involve outlining a ten-year career plan or telling their employer why they had always wanted to work with tuna; it simply required them to throw a fish as far as they could. Those with the strongest arms were hired.

In 1979, two members of the committee for Tunarama – the town's tuna-related festival held each year since 1962 on the weekend around Australia Day, 26 January – witnessed this spectacle and thought that a tuna toss could make for an exciting new event. So it was that hundreds of spectators lined up to watch the town's burliest men – many of them fish workers – stand on a line drawn on the beach and hurl medium-sized, approximately 20-pound tuna into oblivion. All the fish used were frozen to stop them exploding on impact and, because not everyone would be comfortable with handling a dead fish, it was decided that the best method of projection would be to attach the tuna to a rope handle. The first throwers summoned up all their strength and heaved the fish along the beach by way of an inelegant underarm lunge, before a local schoolteacher stepped up to the mark. It so happened that in his younger days John Penny was an accomplished hammer thrower, and, to the amazement of onlookers and the irritation of his fellow competitors, he proceeded to whirl the fish around his head a few times and launch it way into the distance – just like the hammer throw, only smellier. Some cried foul, but the committee saw nothing wrong with his method, and his throw won the day.

As the annual tuna toss grew in popularity, throwers tried to copy Penny's style, certain that it was the way to success. In 1998, another Australian hammer thrower, Sean Carlin, set what still stands as the tuna toss record, a throw of 122 feet. Four years later, hammer thrower Brooke Krueger set the ladies' record with a toss just shy of 70 foot. These fish really can fly, as an unfortunate spectator discovered in 1989, when she was hit by a 17-pound frozen tuna and ended up spending six days in hospital.

Although the fish tossed are considered to be unusable by-catch, being too small for market and not intended for consumption, in 2007 it was decided, in a nod to the green lobby, to use rubberised versions in the trials. However, for the finals, competitors are still allowed to throw real fish, and for youngsters there is the less strenuous prawn toss. In the rest of the world tossed prawn is a salad, but in Port Lincoln it's a sport.

WELLY WANGING WORLD CHAMPIONSHIPS,
UPPERTHONG, WEST YORKSHIRE, ENGLAND

According to Yorkshire folklore, the sport of welly wanging stemmed from an incident in bygone days at a pub in Upperthong when one farmer committed the cardinal sin of accidentally spilling ale into the wellington boot of another. The farmer, whose trousers were soaked and whose boot was filled with ale, was not best pleased and, in a fit of rage, removed the wet welly and chased the clumsy drinker out of the pub, battering him with the boot as an improvised rubber weapon. However, with only one boot to run in, he was not as fast as his prey, so as the altercation spilled out into the lane, he resorted to throwing ('wanging' in Yorkshire parlance) the boot as hard as he could in the direction of the fleeing farmer. It is unclear whether or not he managed to score a direct hit but, in such a close-knit community, the fracas was the talk of the village over the next few weeks and provided such a wealth of entertainment that locals began staging dramatic reconstructions. Eventually someone had the bright idea of staging a competition to see who could throw a wellington boot the greatest distance. A farmers' feud became a fully-fledged sport.

There are four main techniques for ensuring satisfactory welly propulsion. The most common is the one-handed throw where the competitor runs up to the mark, boot held in trailing hand, and then launches it through the air like a javelin, except that no unwitting judge or spectator is ever likely to be skewered by a wellington boot. With a particularly large boot or for someone with small hands, a double-handed throw may be practised, so that both hands can fit securely around the footwear. This is not dissimilar to an Olympic hammer thrower's technique. A popular style for youngsters and beginners is the 'between the legs' throw, where competitors face forwards, bending the legs slightly to accommodate the swing, and release the boot into the air. When swinging back and forth between the legs for extra momentum prior to launch, care must be taken lest the toe of the boot causes a mishap on the forward move. Wangers' groin is an all-too-common injury associated with the sport. The fourth style is the backward throw, in which the boot is hurled over the head while the competitor is facing away from the target area. Although this method allows for a large backswing, it does mean that the target area is out of sight for the duration of the swing. There is also the very real risk of hitting oneself on the head with the boot.

The World Welly Wanging Association, conveniently based in Upperthong rather than, say, Zurich, has laid down strict rules for its championships, which are staged each year in June. The standard welly for use is the Dunlop green size 9, non-steel toecap. Competitors can choose whether they prefer to throw a left or right boot, but the boot must not be tampered with in any way – for example, the leg must not be rolled back on top of the foot. The boot may be thrown either from a standing position or from a run-up not exceeding forty-two paces. This number was chosen in honour of *The Hitchhiker's Guide to the Galaxy* author Douglas Adams, who was apparently something of a connoisseur of the sport. The welly must land within the designated playing area, known as the 'thong'. While it is only natural to wish to take advantage of the prevailing weather conditions, on a windy day throwers may wait no longer than a minute for a suitable gust. Finally, all distances are measured in yards, feet and inches – none of this metric nonsense. In recent years, Adam Taylor has been the wanger to beat, winning the men's title three years in a row from 2013 to 2015.

Many other countries host similar events. Taihape in New Zealand calls itself the gumboot-throwing capital of the world, and annual boot-throwing championships also take place in Germany, Finland, Sweden and Poland. The target that every competitor is trying to beat is the world record of 214 foot 4 inches set by Finland's Jouni Viljanen in 1999. It is doubtful whether that irate Yorkshire farmer achieved anything approaching that distance, but if that was simply because his enemy's head got in the way, he would have been more than satisfied.

WORLD CHAMPIONSHIP COW CHIP THROWING
CONTEST, BEAVER, OKLAHOMA, USA

As we have seen with cow-pat bingo, the emissions from a bovine backside offer no end of sporting possibilities. In Beaver, Oklahoma, where cows used to outnumber humans by sixteen to one, competitors have been throwing dried cow pats (or cow chips) at the annual Cimarron Territory Celebration on the third Saturday in April since 1970. Cow-chip throwing is every bit as keenly contested as the Olympic javelin or shot-put, the only difference being that nobody wants to shake hands afterwards.

The local Chamber of Commerce hit upon the idea of throwing cow crap as a way of spicing up interest in the festival. They took their inspiration from the days when pioneer settlers burned dried buffalo chips as a cheap and abundant source of fuel. The story goes that these pioneers used to play a game with any surplus chips by seeing how far they could toss them into a wagon. So what better way to celebrate the history of Beaver County than with a cow-chip throwing contest whose motto is: 'When the chips are down, pick 'em up and throw 'em!'

Today, competitors travel from as far afield as Australia, Japan and Germany, and mercifully for airport customs staff, they do not need to bring their own cow pats with them. Instead, an official on-site dung wagon supplies the disc-shaped projectiles, which must be at least six inches in diameter. Any competitor who attempts to tamper with a chip to make it more aerodynamic automatically incurs a twenty-five-foot penalty. Novice throwers tend to opt for larger chips in the belief that they will fly further, but wise veterans know that the larger, drier chips often break apart in mid-air, and so they prefer chips that are compact but solid and are as close as possible to being round, as if a cow has just excreted a small discus. Before picking their missile, they shake it to test for durability, because a cow chip that splinters does nobody any favours, especially if the shards blow back into the thrower's face. For this reason, seasoned cow-chip throwers keep their mouths closed on windy days. Competitors are each allowed two throws and are allowed to lick their fingers between throws in order to obtain a better grip on the chip. Many are quite happy to forgo this concession. Given the shape of the chip, the temptation is to throw it Frisbee-style, but those in the know advise an overhand action with a flick of the wrist at the point of release to help counter the persistent plains winds that threaten to carry the chip out of bounds.

The best throw at the contest came in 2015 when Drew Russell hurled his cow chip a distance of 188 foot 6 inches, breaking Robby Deevers' fourteen-year-old record by three feet. Past luminaries include Roy Kygar, who recorded a hat-trick of wins in the late 1980s. There are various other cow-pat throwing contests in the United States – including Wisconsin, Illinois and South Dakota – but any red-blooded male will always head straight for Beaver.

WORLD GRAVY WRESTLING CHAMPIONSHIPS, STACKSTEADS, LANCASHIRE, ENGLAND

Watching a cow wrestle a pregnant nun in a giant bowl of gravy is the type of dream that would keep a psychiatrist in work for months. Yet every August Bank Holiday since 2006, a similar dream has become reality in a corner of Lancashire, where game souls in fancy dress take part in the World Gravy Wrestling Championships.

Just a few miles from the venue of the World Black Pudding Throwing Championships, a plastic-lined pool is set up outside the Rose 'n' Bowl pub and is then filled with 1,000 litres of warm gravy so that wrestlers can grapple in the brown stuff for two minutes in what has been billed 'one of the world's craziest culinary competitions'. Amid all the splashing, much of the gravy becomes displaced and so it has to be topped up regularly throughout the competition. As most of the stock wrestling moves are unachievable by enthusiastic amateurs dressed as Fred Flintstone, Gandalf, a chicken or the aforementioned expectant nun, victory in each bout is largely determined by which fighter earns the greatest applause from the spectators. Just in case anyone does manage a proper wrestling manoeuvre, the scoring system works as follows:

- Three points for a fall, when your opponent is held down in the gravy with both shoulders for a three-second count.
- Two points for a near-fall, when one shoulder is held down in the gravy for a three-second count.
- Two points for a take-down, when your opponent is down in the gravy and you have full control.

- Two points for a reversal, when you are down in the gravy but recover to take control of your opponent.
- One point for an escape, when you are down in the gravy but escape the hold and reach a neutral point in the gravy.
- Up to twenty points can be awarded by the judges for competitors who receive the loudest applause, wear the best costume, or raise the biggest laugh.
- Up to ten penalty points will be deducted for an infraction. These include leaving the paddling pool, jumping on opponents, grabbing an opponent's clothing, unfair use of props and unnecessary roughness.

Referee Stephen Claxon told the *Rossendale Free Press*: 'It's just a crazy, messy and disgusting experience, and as a referee it can get pretty cold and uncomfortable standing in gravy for five hours. The competitors don't hold back either and don't mind beating me up. The most dangerous tend to be the women. They really go for it as they think they can get away with it. Holds and throws are okay but things like gouging and drowning are banned – not that people don't try it though!'

The championships started out as a publicity stunt for the short-lived Pennine Food Festival, but although the festival has faded away, the gravy wrestling has retained its appeal despite losing some of its flavour. That is because the organisers no longer use real gravy, having replaced it with a concoction of cornflour and caramel after the meat content was found to attract wasps. Also, some wrestlers complained of being followed home by packs of dogs. Competitors are now hosed down by the fire brigade after each bout. Charity worker Joel Hicks won the men's title for the third time in 2015, but recent shoulder surgery restricted his movement in 2016 and he missed out to Paddy Sharky.

One of the organisers, Andy Holt, emphasises that it is a fun event and that injuries are rare. 'Two of them ended up in casualty one year,' he told the *Guardian*, 'one dressed as a nun, the other as a goblin. They turned up at reception covered in gravy. The receptionist took one look at them and mistook them for perverts.'

WORLD HAGGIS HURLING CHAMPIONSHIPS, AULDGIRTH, DUMFRIES AND GALLOWAY, SCOTLAND

In 1977, Robin Dunseath and his friends placed an advert in a Scottish national newspaper calling for competitors at the Gathering of the Clans in Edinburgh to revive the seventeenth-century sport of haggis hurling. It was, he said, a sport that had originated among the wives of peat bog workers who, in order to save a long trek, used to throw the cooked lunch of haggis across wet marshland for their menfolk to catch in their kilts. Accuracy was essential as a dropped haggis would mean half an hour or so scraping off clumps of peat from their lunch.

As Mr Dunseath was only too aware, there was no ancient sport of haggis hurling – in 2004, he finally confessed to the hoax, calling it an 'exercise in gullibility' – but the advert attracted so much interest that he felt obliged to invent the sport, along with some rules. The joke is still running forty years on, with the official World Haggis Hurling Championships being staged for years at the end of January in the grounds of Robert Burns' cottage in Ayrshire – a fitting venue for such a stereotypical Scottish pursuit. It was, after all, Burns who wrote *Address to a Haggis*, an ode of appreciation to the Scottish national dish of sheep's heart, liver and lungs, flavoured with oatmeal, onion and suet, all encased in a sheep's stomach. In 2017, the event was moved to another of Burns' homes, Ellisland Farm in Dumfries and Galloway, a setting which inspired some of his most celebrated poems.

In competition, the pre-boiled haggis is hurled from atop a platform – usually a half-barrel of whisky. It requires a subtle technique rather than sheer brute force, as the haggis must still be edible after landing. A split haggis results in instant disqualification. For that reason, it is subjected to close inspection before being thrown to make sure that no alien firming agents have been applied. Marks are awarded for both distance and accuracy. Organiser and regular competitor Stuart Cochrane told *the Scotsman*: 'You have to have a very good sense of balance and be able to pivot quite far so that when you swing your hips and release, then it's got the most momentum. You want the haggis to skim through the air to prevent it from splitting on the ground.'

At the 2011 Bearsden and Milngavie Highland Games, nineteen-year-old Lorne Coltart hurled a 1 lb 8 oz haggis a mighty 217 feet, shattering the world record of 180 foot 10 inches, which had been held by Alan Pettigrew since 1984. In fact Coltart's throw was so huge and unexpected that officials charged with measuring the distance ran out of white tape. To any hurler who can break the record, the world championships offer a prize of a year's supply of haggis, which may be seen by non-Scots as more of a deterrent than a reward.

Robin Dunseath remained president of the World Haggis Hurling Association for twenty years and wrote the definitive book on the subject, titled *The Complete Haggis Hurler*, all the proceeds going to charity. His prank developed such a life of its own that haggis hurling has become a bona fide sport in many countries where Scots have settled. However, even he could not have foreseen some of the controversy it would arouse in distant lands. Plans to use a fake haggis in a hurling competition at a Highland festival in Melbourne, Australia split the purists from those who were fearful of the mess caused by an exploding sheep's stomach. The idea was to create a simulated haggis in the form of a bag packed with sand or oatmeal, but as one diehard, butcher Rob Boyle, said witheringly: 'If there's no haggis, how can it be haggis hurling? I'm a traditionalist. If you have an egg-and-spoon race you don't use a golf ball.'

Meanwhile Perth, Ontario stages the **Canadian Haggis Hurling Championship**, held in conjunction with the **Perth Kilt Run**, an eight-kilometre race in which all the athletes wear kilts.

WORLD PILLOW FIGHT CHAMPIONSHIPS,
SONOMA COUNTY, CALIFORNIA, USA

While the sport of pillow fighting may have had its origins in English public schools after lights out in the dorm with Ffffitch-Harris trying to knock ten bells of excrement out of Fanshawe Minor, the world championships stemmed not from a desire for revenge over who snitched about putting a live frog down Matron's bloomers, but from a practical need to raise funds for the small country town of Kenwood in Sonoma County, California. Back in 1964, two local community groups held charitable functions to this end, one of which was the World Pillow Fight Championships. A steel pole was erected across Los Guillicos Spring Creek, the creek was filled with mud and the Blue Riband event of international pillow fighting was born.

The combatants climb on to the twenty-eight-foot-long stainless steel pole at either end and, in a sitting position, slide their way along to the centre. They then proceed to whack each other with their pillows. The pole rolls freely during bouts, so staying on it is a major problem, even for the winner. Consequently, fights rarely last more than a few seconds and both fighters invariably fall into the three-foot-deep mud bath. Bouts are decided on the best of three falls. It is a test of strength and balance.

The world championships progressed from a small local affair to a major spectacle attracting up to ten thousand people. One of the highlights was in 1980 when comedians Tommy and Dick Smothers (together the Smothers Brothers) slid out to the pole's centre and swatted each other with increasing ferocity. Tommy, a Kenwood resident, won but both ended up in the mud pit, to the delight of the crowd. Ultimately, however, Kenwood became a victim of its own success. By 2006, the event had become too big for the town, and the championships were discontinued until September 2014, when they returned at a new, larger venue at Sonoma Mountain Village. Also returning in 2014 was sixty-three-year-old veteran pillow fighter Jerry McEntire Sr, who had won the world title in the 1970s, 1980s and 1990s. 'This is my thirty-fourth year,' he told the local *Press Democrat* newspaper. 'I intend to keep going until I can claim forty years of pillow fighting.' Who wouldn't want to be able to lay claim to that?

With the uncertainty surrounding the California competition, pillow fighters feared that there would be no outlet for their soft-centred aggression. For some, it was a real downer. In a bid to fill the gap, in 2011 New York City staged the first **Pillow Fight World Cup**. There were no slippery poles or mud pits – instead women stepped into a boxing ring and fought each other with pillows over the course of two, two-minute rounds. Judges awarded points for hits to the head and body, and penalised fighters for turning their back on their opponent or for dropping to their knees. Austrian pillow fighter Maylin Kretzschmar told the *Huffington Post*: 'It is less brutal than boxing, but you still need technique. It's a fun sport. I don't want to punch someone in the face, but you can still get rid of your aggression.' At the end of the tournament, her fellow Austrian, Gudrun Grondinger, was crowned pillow-fighting queen of the world. There might not have been many feathers left in her pillow, but at least she now had one in her cap.

WORLD TOE WRESTLING CHAMPIONSHIP,
FENNY BENTLEY, DERBYSHIRE, ENGLAND

Alan 'Nasty' Nash is not a man with whom you would wish to cross swords, or even worse, toes. For the father of four from Weston Coyney, Staffordshire is the self-confessed bad boy of international toe wrestling, but backs up his uncompromising attitude with undeniable talent in the foot department. He was crowned world champion for the tenth time in 2013 after going toe-to-toe with twenty other competitors at the annual World Toe Wrestling Championship at the Bentley Brook Inn at Fenny Bentley, near Ashbourne in Derbyshire.

The event was introduced to the sporting calendar in 1976 when four regulars at the Royal Oak in nearby Wetton decided to invent a sport at which the British could be the best in the world. Unfortunately a Canadian won and took the trophy home with him, so the contest was dropped for eighteen years until the Brits had regrouped.

As with most combat sports, the wrestlers undergo a medical beforehand. All toes must be thoroughly examined and passed by a qualified nurse before their owners are allowed to compete. No fungal infections are permitted nor feet so pungent that they cause the nurse to faint. Nails must be neatly trimmed. Following the opening call to remove shoes and socks, competitors sit barefoot facing each other and lock their big toes together, the object being to pin their opponent's big toe on the platform (or toedium) for three seconds in a best-of-three contest. The first round is fought with right feet, the second with left, and the third (if necessary) is fought with right feet again. While putting their best foot forward, competitors must keep their hands flat on the floor and their non-fighting foot in the air. Shifting position to gain leverage is strictly prohibited. As the referee warns: 'The crack of your bottom must remain flush with the line at all times.'

Psychology plays a key role for these podiatric gladiators. Contests begin with a blood-curdling chant as the rivals get themselves into the zone, sometimes threatening, 'I'll break your ankle' or delivering the ultimate toe wrestling insult, 'Lick my verruca!' Nash, the bald beast, lifted the title at his first attempt in 1994 and has dominated the event ever since. His finest hour came in 1997 when, after suffering four dislocated toes in the semi-final, he rested them in an ice bucket before simply snapping them back into place and winning the final. 'I just don't like losing,' he said with a degree of understatement. He trains at the gym three times a week and owes his toe strength to a diet of raw meat. 'I don't eat fruit or vegetables,' he once told ESPN. 'If it was meant to be eaten, it wouldn't be buried in the ground.' In a more serious vein, he adds: 'The sport is like arm wrestling, but you use your legs instead. However, it is harder than arm wrestling because you need to have strength in your whole body to be good at it. My technique is to hurt the first person that comes up against me: hurt them bad and terrify everyone else.'

For years, Nash's arch-rival was Paul 'Predatoe' Beech (formerly known as 'The Toeminator'), and there was no shortage of bad blood between the pair after Beech defeated Nash in 2011. Nash claimed Beech employed illegal moves and that at one point his non-wrestling foot dropped on the floor instead of being suspended above the toedium. Beech responded by threatening to break Nash's ankle if he returned the following year. There was trouble afoot.

When Nash's toes finally retire to pursue more leisurely activities such as walking to the pub, his son Aaron 'Toerannosaurus' Nash, who has already gained a foothold in the sport, is ready to assume the family mantle. You have been warned.

CHAPTER SEVEN

BOGGED DOWN

MUD OLYMPICS, BRUNSBÜTTEL, GERMANY

It is perhaps surprising that it took analytical German minds to conclude that what the Olympic Games, the world's greatest all-round sporting event – the one that had brought us Paavo Nurmi, Jesse Owens and Mark Spitz – really needed to spice things up was mud. Dirty, squelchy mud, and lots of it. How much more dramatic, they reasoned, would the Olympic 100 metres be if all the athletes were obliged to wear gumboots? How long would the marathon take if everyone was knee-deep in clinging, cloying mud? And what about the hop, step and sink? They realised they were on to something.

It all started out in 1978 as little more than a jolly romp in the mud among friends before being revived and expanded in 2004 by local artist Jens Rusch, who, following a long battle with illness, saw the Mud Olympics as a way of raising money for cancer charities. The *Wattolümpiade* or Mud Olympics now take place annually on the vast expanse of black mud flats that line the estuary of the River Elbe where it flows out into the North Sea near Hamburg. The motto of the Games is 'dirty sport for a clean cause'. Some 500 people compete in the various disciplines, which include mud volleyball, mud soccer, mud handball, sledge racing, the long-distance rubber boot toss, and *tampentrecken*, a tug-of-war contest in which the heavyweight competitors regularly experience that sinking feeling. There is also a relay race where, in keeping with the location, runners – or more accurately, squelchers – hand over a fake eel rather than a baton. The Games are staged as part of a summer weekend festival featuring local bands, called Mudstock.

The tide is only out for four hours, so the sports events have a limited duration. For example, mud volleyball matches last just seven minutes, but that is ample time for the players – all of whom wear fancy dress for the occasion – to get thoroughly filthy. Win or lose, they all go home happy. 'Seven minutes in the mud are like seven days' holiday,' says one.

The coveted Mud Olympics trophy is awarded to the winners of each contest, as well as to the funniest team, the best fan club, and the best costume. Each participant also receives a medal to remind them of their time at the *Wattolümpiade*. They must get another reminder every time they wash their hair for the following fortnight.

SWAMP SOCCER WORLD CHAMPIONSHIPS, HYRYNSALMI, FINLAND

Those of a certain age will recall how Football League matches in Britain used to be played on something resembling a swamp week in, week out through the winter months. Shirt numbers would be obliterated by a layer of mud, the ball would stick in a giant puddle in the goalmouth, and sliding tackles would end up in the main stand. Those halcyon days have been brought back to life by the sport of swamp soccer, where players wade about in mud that can be anything from six to twenty-four inches deep. The pitches look more like pig pens than fields of sporting excellence.

The game was devised in Finland when cross-country skiers who were training in the swamps became bored and decided to stage a soccer tournament. The first organised event was the 1998 Finnish championship, the brainchild of Jyrki Väänänen, who duly became known as the 'Swamp Baron', and this was followed two years later by the inaugural Swamp Soccer World Championships on Vuorisuo Bog in Hyrynsalmi, some 400 miles north-east of Helsinki. They have been staged there annually ever since, attracting as many as three hundred teams from ten different countries. The two-day tournament takes place in July on twenty pitches, and during the competition almost a thousand games are played.

Matches are six-a-side and are played over two halves of ten minutes on pitches that are about half the size of a standard soccer pitch. The pitch markings take the form of yellow plastic bands. Players can be substituted as often as necessary, which, given the game's stamina-sapping nature, is every few minutes. They are strongly advised to tape their footwear in place for fear of seeing their boots sucked down into the mud. There is no offside rule, and kick-offs, penalties, corners and throw-ins are taken by dropping the ball on to a player's foot. Passing is at a premium. 'It doesn't matter how you play on grass, when you get on that mud it's completely different,' says a leading player. 'There is very little skill involved. You just go for it – head towards goal. The running bit's not too bad – it's getting the ball to keep up with you that isn't so easy.'

The FIFA of swamp football is Swamp Soccer UK, based in Scotland, and its showpiece event is the **Swamp Soccer World Cup**, which, after being staged in Scotland since 2006 (often at Blairmore, Argyll in the Scottish Highlands), has recently spread its wings to China and Turkey. Competing teams have included Mudchesthair United and Real Mudrid.

Swamp Soccer UK founder Stewart Miller says of the game: 'It basically turns the whole competitive sporting concept on its head, in that the playing surface is deliberately poor and you don't have to be a supreme athlete to take part. The majority of teams participate purely for fun and the opportunity to roll around in the muck. It's not so much about the winning – in fact, the only real way of spotting the champions is by the amount of mud on them. I've had players inform me that they have found dirt in places that they would never have imagined, many days after the event.'

WORLD BOG SNORKELLING CHAMPIONSHIPS, LLANWRTYD WELLS, POWYS, WALES

For most snorkellers, the dream experience involves crystal-clear tropical waters, brightly coloured fish, beautiful coral reefs, and the sun's rays bearing down on the shoulders – not standing chest deep in freezing cold, murky water in the middle of a Welsh field with only leeches for company. Welcome to the world of bog snorkelling, an event that is possibly even less glamorous than it sounds.

The World Bog Snorkelling Championships have been staged at the Waen Rhydd peat bog near the Welsh town of Llanwrtyd Wells every year since 1985, and like the area's other sporting claim to fame, The Man Versus Horse Marathon, it was devised by local landlord Gordon Green to put the town on the tourist map. Wearing a mask, snorkel, flippers, fancy dress and usually a wetsuit, more than a hundred and fifty competitors a year (from as far afield as Australia, New Zealand, the United States, Canada, Germany, Sweden and the Czech Republic) snorkel two lengths of a specially dug sixty-yard-long, four-foot-deep trench which runs through a weed-infested peat bog. Conventional swimming strokes such as the breaststroke and crawl are banned, so the participants must rely on flipper power alone. With underwater visibility practically zero, it has been compared to swimming through pea soup.

Competitors say the most disgusting part is the taste of the bog water. The rest is exhausting but strangely exhilarating. 'You just put your head down and paddle those legs like crazy,' said one. The ideal attributes for a bog snorkeller are reckoned to be stamina, buoyancy and an ability to pick a path through the reeds. Not drowning also helps.

The world bog snorkelling record was set in 2016 at the Irish Bog Snorkelling Championships by Paddy Lambe, who navigated the mud and water of the stench trench in a time of 1 minute 19 seconds – several seconds faster than the bog standard. The fastest time at the world championships is 1 minute 22.56 seconds and was set by former Surrey club swimmer Kirsty Johnson in 2014. In doing so, Johnson put an end to the winning run of Irish teenager Dineka Maguire, who had taken the women's title for the previous four years.

So popular has bog snorkelling become that Llanwrtyd Wells also hosts a spin-off event – the **World Mountain Bike Bog Snorkelling Championships**, where competitors cycle along a forty-five-yard-long, six-foot-deep peat bog. The bikes have water-filled tyres so that they can grip the bottom of the bog and the cyclists wear lead-weighted belts to prevent them floating off their bikes.

These two events plus the bog snorkelling triathlon (a run, a bog snorkel, and a bike ride), take place over the August Bank Holiday weekend and make up what is known as the 'bog weekender', a phrase more readily associated with a bad dose of gastro-enteritis. The date has been carefully chosen because, as everyone in the UK knows, it always rains on a Bank Holiday. And a prolonged downpour makes for ideal bog snorkelling conditions.

CHAPTER EIGHT

CHILLING OUT

BARSTOOL SKI RACING, MARTIN CITY, MONTANA, USA

Nobody who has ever contemplated riding a barstool down a hill will be surprised to learn that the sport of barstool ski racing was born out of prodigious quantities of alcohol. It is said to have originated in 1978 at the Belton Chalet bar at West Glacier near Martin City, Montana, when two skiers walked in and tried to talk a group of venerable drinkers into going out skiing. One of the old-timers replied: 'The day you put skis on this barstool is the day I'll go skiing with you!'

The skiers saw this as a challenge, and it wasn't long before the sozzled seniors were sliding down a nearby hill on their barstools, beer in hand. What started with eight makeshift sledges has evolved into a weekend-long competition every February in which dozens of competitors race each other two at a time down a snow-covered hill on barstools, beer barrels, boats, milk cans, picnic tables, and basically anything to which skis can be attached. The object is to be the first to make it to the bottom, ideally without falling off, although when riding a barstool downhill at speed, that can be a tall order.

Stools are divided into two categories – basic and steerable. With the former, you just point yourself towards the bottom of the hill, hold on for dear life and hope for the best. Stools that can be steered – usually with the addition of a steering wheel – are for more seriously minded competitors, although in barstool ski racing the term is relative. In both cases, the rules state that the stool must be ridden 'sitting down, in a drinking position, with the rider's butt on the stool'. Every other means of descent goes into the 'anything goes' division. This includes the stripper pole that was once ridden down the hill by a female competitor in her forties. Her choice of transport was actually quite appropriate because the summit of the racing slope is called Sugar Hill, so named because there used to be a brothel at the top, where local men went to get some sugar. At least that was their story. At the start line at the top of the hill, riders can either push themselves or acquire the services of a pusher for extra momentum. Qualifying races take place on the Saturday and again on the Sunday morning, with the finals on Sunday afternoon for anyone who is still sober.

Among the entrants in 2016 was seventy-one-year-old Nancy McDowell, who was inspired to race after receiving a medical stand with an attached toilet seat for her seventieth birthday. She had the joke gift converted into a sledge, fixed panties to the back, and sailed down the hill to supportive cries of 'Go granny, go!'

But it's the humble barstool that is the foundation of the sport – an item of furniture designed ironically to stop movement (away from the bar) having now been converted into a veritable racing machine for the fearless and foolhardy.

ICE CRICKET WORLD CUP, TALLINN, ESTONIA

Ask any English ex-pat what they miss most about their homeland and they will invariably come up with something along the lines of tea, pubs and cricket. The weather, rush-hour traffic, knife crime and Katie Hopkins rarely get a mention. When Jason Barry moved to Estonia, he was determined to increase the popularity of cricket in that country and to turn it into a year-round sport. Accordingly, he organised an international cricket championship there – but not on grass, on ice. It has since developed into the Ice Cricket World Cup, played annually in winter on the frozen Lake Harku in the capital, Tallinn, where temperatures can dip as low as minus 25°C. It is the only form of cricket where making a diving catch can result in a mouthful of wet snow.

Barry told the *Baltic Times*: 'I got the idea from seeing the ice fishermen on the lake each year and wondered if it would be possible to use this 'temporary sports arena' for taking away the winter boredom. It turned out to be perfect.'

The wicket for the tournament is painstakingly carved into the ice, leaving a snow-covered outfield, and the boundary is marked off to keep bewildered locals at bay. The last thing a fielder needs as he waits under a lofted on-drive is to see a skier coming at him out of the corner of his eye or to disappear down an ice fisherman's hole. No matting is used for the actual wicket, so the bounce and trajectory are solely dependent on the ice. Games are six-a-side (so that fielders are always on the move) and consist of six overs per innings to ensure that everyone gets a chance to bowl. A composite plastic red ball is used, similar to the type used in indoor cricket, as a traditional leather ball would freeze and harden in the icy temperatures. Fours and sixes are scored as per usual with boundary shots, while local rules dictate that an extra six runs should be added to the batsman's total if his shot hits a passing moose.

Even though the players often wear spikes to improve their footing, it is hard for bowlers to avoid slipping and sliding their way to the crease. Suffice to say that run-ups tend to be on the short side – no one tries to emulate the pace of Dennis Lillee or Michael Holding. Players wear gloves, hats and a range of warm knitwear. Some less hardy souls even don jackets, regardless of the fact that bulky clothing tends to hinder stroke play. Nobody wears whites, simply because they could be lost for days in the outfield. Meanwhile, the one thing that neither team wants is a wicket that is starting to turn, because in ice cricket it can mean that it is starting to turn to slush.

The first Ice Cricket World Championship, as it was then known, was held in 2007 and was played in a round-robin format. Jason Barry captained the Estonian team, but two English teams – Polygon from Surrey and Upminster Seconds from Essex – ended up tying for first place. Thus there was no outright winner. It could only happen in cricket. Subsequent champions have come from Gibraltar, England and Australia.

Although Estonia is now acknowledged as the Mecca of ice cricket, the first regular tournament was played in the elegant Swiss alpine resort of St Moritz in 1988, when a group of British cricketers challenged the students of the international boarding school Lyceum Alpinum Zuoz to a game. It has since grown into an annual event, the **Cricket On Ice Trophy**: a twenty-over round-robin contest played over three days in February on the frozen Lake St Moritz. This is T20 cricket on ice. The big differences with the Estonian competition are that a strip of artificial turf is laid down as the wicket, the players wear more traditional cricketing apparel, and they use an orange rubber ball. Every year, four teams are invited, regular participants being the Old Cholmeleians, the old boys of Highgate School.

The occasion has attracted international players. Indeed, the most dramatic moment in the history of Swiss ice cricket occurred in January 1990 when English cricketer David Gower parked his rental car on the ice, but was unlucky enough to choose a relatively thin spot. Overnight, the ice broke and his car sank.

SHOVEL RACING WORLD CHAMPIONSHIPS, ANGEL
FIRE RESORT, SANTA FE, NEW MEXICO, USA

One day, workers at the Angel Fire Ski Resort in northern New Mexico discovered that they could move around the slopes much faster at the end of their shift if, instead of carrying their large snow shovels, they rode them instead. It didn't take long for the competitive juices to start flowing and by 1975 organised snow shovel races were being staged regularly at the resort. This in turn led to the Shovel Racing World Championships.

The concept is simple: riders lie down on a standard, unmodified aluminium shovel, handle pointing downhill, feet facing forward, then grab the handle in front of them and speed down the mountain as fast as they can. Hitting speeds of 70mph on the 1,000-foot course, the quickest can make the descent in a little over thirteen seconds. Some don't make it that far, ending up in an ungainly heap in the snow partway down. For that reason, helmets are compulsory, but it is not only the impact with the mountain that shovellers have to beware of; an uncontrolled collision between any of the more delicate parts of the body and the shovel handle is definitely not advisable.

The sport reached the peak of its popularity in 1997 when it was included in the Winter X Games, a showcase for extreme winter sports. However, a serious injury to John 'Shovelmeister' Strader during a high-speed crash led the organisers to decide that shovel racing was too extreme even for them, and the fledgling event was dropped. At that time, many racers modified their shovels in the search for ever greater speed. Some of these pimped-up shovels looked more like space rockets, but after one mishap too many in 2005, the competition was cancelled at Angel Fire for five years due to safety concerns. The very future of the sport looked to be in jeopardy. When it eventually returned in 2010, all modified shovels were banned, so that only standard shovels were allowed in competition. The only additions permitted are paint, a wax covering on the underside to reduce friction, and a layer of adhesive tape on the handle to make it easier to grip. Snow shovel racing had gone back to basics.

Nowadays more than a hundred competitors take to the slopes every February in seven different categories based on age, gender and skill level. The winner in each division is the one with the fastest combined time over two runs, with even the youngest children between the ages of six and nine being able to reach speeds in excess of 40mph. Snow shovel racing has earned a reprieve, but the general feeling is that it is not so much the sport the Winter Olympics forgot; it is the one that it wisely chose to ignore.

If you can't make it to New Mexico, you could try riding your garden spade down the slope next to your potting shed, but it is unlikely that it will achieve the same effect.

UNDERWATER ICE HOCKEY WORLD
CUP, WEISSENSEE, AUSTRIA

For Austrian freediver and extreme sports enthusiast Christian Redl, underwater hockey – or octopush – where players manoeuvre a puck across the floor of a swimming pool, simply wasn't weird enough. He wanted to take things a step further, so he developed underwater ice hockey (sometimes called sub-aqua ice hockey), which is played beneath a frozen lake, pond or swimming pool with all the participants performing upside down.

Descending through holes carved out of the ice, the players wear diving masks, fins and wetsuits and, wielding hockey sticks, use the underside of the frozen surface as the playing area for a ten-inch puck. This is made of styrofoam so that rather than sinking, it floats right beneath the ice. Instead of having breathing apparatus, the players come to the surface for air every thirty to sixty seconds and swap places with a team-mate. Consequently one of the chief requirements of an underwater ice hockey player is to know where the holes in the ice are.

As might be expected, the game is not quite as brutal as ice hockey that is played the right way up and on the other side of the ice. For one thing, there are only two players on each team, so the scope for a mass brawl is limited. The rink measures six metres wide by eight metres long, and the nets are fastened to the ice cover upside down. Each of the three periods lasts ten minutes with two ten-minute breaks in between to allow the players to warm up in a sauna. Spectators watch the action on monitors above ground.

Functioning upside down often leads to the players becoming disoriented underwater, and if they spend too long beneath the surface and do not reach the air hole in time, they can suffer blackouts. In case of mishaps, games are supervised by four trained divers with oxygen tanks.

The first Underwater Ice Hockey World Cup was held at Weissensee, Austria in February 2007. Eight European countries were represented, with Finland eventually emerging victorious ahead of Austria and Slovakia. The second World Cup was staged at the same venue in 2013, and this time the host nation triumphed. One of the biggest challenges with staging a major underwater ice hockey tournament is finding a location where the ice is thick enough to hold the weight of all the spectators and safety officials.

Organiser Redl told the *Daily Mail*: 'After diving a lot under ice, I wondered which sports had the potential to be played underneath ice, and that's when the game was born. The matches are very fast paced, so the amount of time that divers are under the water is not that long – plus the water is extremely cold.' Before you think of trying it, don't forget this is 'extremely cold' by Austrian standards, a temperature low enough to strike fear into brass monkeys the world over.

WHITE TURF HORSE RACES, ST MORITZ, SWITZERLAND

Not content with ice cricket and ice polo tournaments, every February St Moritz stages a series of horse races on a frozen lake covered with six inches of snow. The White Turf meetings take place on three successive Sundays and draw total crowds of around thirty-five thousand people.

Competing in flat, hurdle and trotting races, the horses wear special shoes with two studs at the back and a toe grip at the front. The jockeys also have extra protection and face the occupational hazard of being blinded by a blizzard whenever the horse in front kicks up snow.

Arguably the most spectacular events at White Turf are the unique skijöring races, where, instead of sitting on top of the horses, the jockeys are pulled behind them on skis. They grip long reins attached to the unsaddled thoroughbreds and are towed around the track for nearly two miles at speeds of over 30mph amid a constant fear of being trampled upon. To reduce that risk, they travel on coloured skis so that the horses can spot them more easily in the snow. Fortunately for the skiers who are being dragged behind, instances of horses defecating mid-race are rare. The start is a particularly tense affair as the reins can easily become tangled or horses can decide to set off in any direction they choose. At the 1965 event, not a single skier managed to cross the finish line. According to skijöring historian Corinne Schlatter, the ideal requisites for a jockey/skier are 'strength, athleticism, balance, instinct, toughness, and a certain degree of foolhardiness'. The person who racks up the most skijöring points over the course of the three Sundays claims the title 'King of the Engadine', St Moritz being located in the Engadine Valley.

The practice of skijöring originated in Scandinavia some 700 years ago as a means of transport during the winter months. One of the first competitive skijöring events was a six-mile road race in 1906 from St Moritz to Champfèr and back. Thirteen competitors started at one-minute intervals and Philip Mark, President of the Alpina Ski Club, and his chestnut gelding Blitz were the fastest, recording a time of twenty minutes twenty-two seconds. The following year saw the first horse races on the lake, including trotting races using sledges, and in 1908, a six-race meeting was introduced at which spectators could place official bets. Its popularity saw the programme extended to three racing days in 1910, allowing for the addition of flat racing (1911) and steeplechasing (1922).

Although the ice on Lake St Moritz is usually at least two feet thick in February, making it strong enough to bear the weight of galloping horses, accidents can happen, and in 2017, British flat jockey George Baker ended up in intensive care following a three-horse pile-up after a crack appeared in the ice 150 yards from the finish line, causing water to come up and undermine the racetrack. It was a harsh reminder that in sport class is permanent, but form and frozen racetracks are temporary.

WORLD ICE GOLF CHAMPIONSHIP, UUMMANNAQ, GREENLAND

As well as being the only golf tournament in the world where your ball is likely to be stolen by a polar bear, the World Ice Golf Championship is also the only one that is likely to be cancelled because the weather is too warm. For a rarely reported effect of climate change is that it poses a serious threat to this illustrious event, which has been staged intermittently on a frozen Greenland fjord since 1999. The course is re-formed each year according to the ice patterns in the fjord, but has had to be cancelled a number of times in its short history because of unseasonal warmth.

The championship was founded by a local hotel owner, Arne Niemann, a man who had never actually played golf but had seen it on TV back in his native Denmark, and it takes the form of a thirty-six-hole contest played over two days. The nine-hole course – at the town of Uummannaq 350 miles inside the Arctic Circle on Greenland's north-west coast – is laid out on the fjord ice a week before the tournament, its shape determined by the location of the shifting icebergs. The fjord remains frozen between November and May, leaving an area of more than five miles available for the yearly construction of the course.

The surface is rough and uneven, ranging from thick ice covered by a thin layer of powdery snow to bare, rock-hard ice. Icebergs are treated as 'ground under repair', and, as such, any player whose ball lands within ten yards of one is given a free drop. This is to prevent the risk of them falling through the thinner, less stable ice that surrounds the bergs. Meanwhile the best way to get out of any of the snow bunkers is with an ice pick rather than a sand wedge.

Ice golfers play with fluorescent orange balls and the greens are, for obvious reasons, called 'whites'. As these are decidedly challenging by nature, players are allowed to smooth over their putts with brooms and the holes are two and a half times bigger than on traditional greens. Golfers often shy away from using clubs with graphite shafts because these may shatter in the cold. Golf carts and trolleys are banned on the course, forcing players to trudge through the snow carrying their bags, making this a test of stamina and endurance as well as skill. Snow blindness may also present a problem during the round, and players are advised to watch each other for signs of frostbite and to be careful not to step into seal holes. This is not a warning you would expect to find at Wentworth.

Professionals and amateurs alike have competed in the event, all agreeing that it is certainly different to routine golf. 'I imagine it's what it's like playing golf on the moon,' said one. Those used to playing in T-shirts on the European or American tours find that their fluency of swing tends to be restricted by the necessity to wear layers of thermal clothing in temperatures that can plummet to minus 25°C even in March.

The future of the World Ice Golf Championship will ultimately be determined by the twenty-first-century climate and whether or not Arctic temperatures rise as much as some experts predict. If their worst fears are realised, the tournament appears to be skating on very thin ice.

WORLD WOK RACING CHAMPIONSHIPS, GERMANY/AUSTRIA

The never-ending battle for Saturday night ratings has been responsible for many crimes against television. These dire and increasingly desperate light entertainment formats have repeatedly presented a platform for celebrity nonentities, pub singers who are told they are stars for occasionally hitting the right note, and, of course, Mr Blobby. An eminently forgettable Saturday night show from the 1990s was *You Bet!*, presented first by Bruce Forsyth and later by Matthew Kelly, which was based on a German show, *Wetten, dass . . .?* If you were lucky enough to miss it, the idea was for members of the public to perform wacky challenges that they had practised endlessly beforehand. Unfortunately none of these included deflating Mr Blobby. The German version featured rather more daring stunts and led to the creation of a new sport in which participants speed down an Olympic bobsled track in a Chinese cooking wok. As with lingerie football, it is the sort of idea that could thrive only inside the head of a TV executive.

Having seen wok racing on *Wetten, dass . . .?*, German TV host and entertainer Stefan Raab quickly saw its potential, and in 2003 the first World Wok Racing Championships were broadcast from Winterburg in Germany. They created quite a stir – not least because one racer sustained a broken arm – and who should take first place but Raab himself? They have since been held annually at various German bobsled tracks and at Innsbruck in Austria. Competitors are a mixture of minor celebrities and professional athletes, including three-time Olympic luge champion Georg Hackl. Unsurprisingly, the German has been crowned world individual wok-racing champion nine times, making him by far the most successful wok racer in history. Analysts agree that the two chief requisites for a great wok racer are nerve and a hard bottom.

There are timed races for one-person and four-person woks, the latter consisting of two pairs of connected woks held together in a frame. The Jamaican bobsled team of *Cool Runnings* fame took part one year. The woks used for racing are the standard cooking vessels with a few modifications. The bottom is reinforced with an epoxy filling and the edges of the wok are coated with polyurethane foam to reduce injuries. To improve performance, the undersides of the woks are polished obsessively and are often heated with a blowtorch before the race. To reduce friction further and to maintain the kitchen theme, the competitors sometimes wear ladles beneath their feet. They also wear helmets and heavy protective clothing, similar to that of ice hockey players, because it can be a sobering thought to realise that all that stands between your body and the rock-hard ice is a frying pan. In any case, the four-person woks can hit speeds of over 70mph. That is seriously fast food.

CHAPTER NINE

ALL CREATURES GREAT AND SMALL

AUSTRALIA DAY COCKROACH RACES,
BRISBANE, QUEENSLAND, AUSTRALIA

The average cockroach can move at fifty body lengths per second, which, in human terms, is equivalent to a speed of 200mph. So it was almost inevitable that someone somewhere would think there was money to be made from betting on the fastest. That moment occurred in 1982 at the Story Bridge Hotel in Brisbane, Australia, when a couple of barflies, fortified by beer, boasted that the cockroaches from their suburb were the quickest in Brisbane. The unusual argument was resolved in the car park the next day – with insects rather than fists – and a cockroach race has been staged at the hotel every year since on Australia Day (26 January). Cockroach racing may lack the natural spectacle of the Cheltenham Gold Cup, but the betting on the outcome is every bit as keen.

Billed as 'the greatest gathering of thoroughbred cockroaches in the world', race day takes place in a thirteen-foot-diameter circular ring. The roaches, each with numbers painted on their backs, are brought into the arena to the sound of bagpipes, introduced by name and then released from a glass bottle into the centre of the ring. Whichever one scuttles to the edge of the ring first is declared the winner. For some roaches, it's their first time out from under the fridge, so they can freeze on the big occasion, but others show no such inhibitions. It is all over in a matter of seconds, and with cockroaches running in all directions, it is no easy matter for the stewards to decide which is the winner. Photo-finish technology may need to be introduced in future. Some of the runners evade capture at the end of the contest and head off among the hundreds of spectators, to the sound of female squeals followed by the crunching of a male foot. For a racing cockroach, an illustrious career can come to a swift, undignified end.

As well as thirteen flat races, there is a steeplechase event, in which the insects have to climb over a length of garden hose which spirals around the ring. Owners can either buy a roach for five dollars on the day or hunt out their own at the kitchen of the nearest dodgy fast food establishment. Try and get there before the pest control officers. Those experienced in the art of roach racing reckon that feeding them biscuits and chocolate builds up their speed. The winning owner receives a $200 voucher to spend in the pub and the honour of serving as a Cockroach Racing Ambassador for the following year's competition.

As with champion racehorses and greyhounds, victorious vermin have been inducted into cockroach racing's Hall of Fame. So let's hear it for, among others, Cocky Balboa, Cocky Dundee, My Fair Cock, and Priscilla, Queen of the Drains.

CAMEL WRESTLING CHAMPIONSHIP, SELÇUK, TURKEY

Before anyone jumps to the conclusion that camel wrestling is insanely ambitious, it should be pointed out that this is not a sport where humans wrestle camels; it is one in which camels wrestle each other – essentially when one male camel gets the hump with a rival. The camels fight by using their necks as leverage to force their opponent to the ground, and the contest is over when one of the camels falls or flees. Although the camels rarely come to any harm, the sport has been declared barbaric and cruel by animal rights campaigners. However, it continues to thrive in the Aegean region of western Turkey, the justification being that it is part of local culture.

Male camels wrestle naturally in the wild, usually over a female in mating season in the same way that stags rut. Around 2,400 years ago, ancient Turkic tribes witnessed this behaviour and began organising camel wrestling contests. These continued sporadically into the twentieth century, and although previous Turkish governments had tried to discourage the sport, since the 1980s it has enjoyed an upsurge in popularity as representing Turkish tradition. Today there are approximately thirty annual festivals in Aegean Turkey between November and March – one of the biggest being at Selçuk – and an estimated two thousand wrestling (or Tulu) camels are bred specially for competition. A successful wrestling camel can sell for over $20,000 and sizeable bets are placed on the outcome of the fights, which have been likened to sumo wrestling with spit.

The bull camels used to be motivated to fight in response to a female in heat being led before them, but this practice has become less common in recent times because it made the animals too aggressive. No owner wants to risk actually losing a prized camel in a fight. The bouts last for up to five minutes, but most end in a tie without any outright winner. Biting is forbidden, and the fight is broken up if either camel sinks its considerable gnashers into its opponent. In an attempt to prevent them doing so, they wear tight halters. Fighting tactics vary. Some camels simply try to trip their opponent with a foot (a move called *cengelci*), while others push their rival to force a retreat (*tekci*). The even-toed ungulate equivalent of a pin fall is the *bagci*, where camels trap their opponent's head under their chest and then try to sit. Camels begin their fighting career at the age of ten and some continue for over a decade. Owners decorate their camels with ornate saddles and often name them after politicians. One look at Nigel Farage and you will understand why.

The events are regularly staged on Sundays in football stadiums and many are preceded by a camel beauty contest, although it is hard to imagine that a camel might lose its looks in the ring. The fights pose dangers not only for the camels but sometimes for the spectators, too, especially if the vanquished camel tries to flee through the crowd hotly pursued by the victor. There is also the ever-present risk of being drenched by flying camel spittle, and, as tempers become frayed over lost wagers, fights occasionally break out between rival owners. Camel meat is often served to spectators at these festivals – a stark reminder, perhaps, of what can happen to a perpetual loser. There is no room for an Eddie the Eagle character in camel wrestling.

DACHSHUND DASH, PORT FAIRY, VICTORIA, AUSTRALIA

Dachshunds aren't built for speed any more than hippos are built for ballet dancing. Their job is to dive down holes and hunt out badgers and other burrow-dwelling animals – that is why the Almighty gave them such long bodies and short legs. However, even though the dachshund was pretty low down on the list when it came to selecting a breed of dog to chase a mechanical hare around a track for a few laps, they have a surprisingly nimble turn of foot and are capable of reaching speeds of 18mph. This is only 5mph slower than Usain Bolt averages for the 100 metres, although surely a dachshund's only chance of coming close to matching him for speed over such a distance would be to take a lump out of his ankle at the start. Since 2007, this hidden athletic ability has encouraged sausage dog owners in the Australian town of Port Fairy to stage an annual race in June, where the pets compete in a series of 'low jump' and sprint contests to determine Victoria's speediest dachshund.

The Dachshund Dash (or Wiener 500 as it is affectionately known) is the Melbourne Cup for dogs with stumpy legs, and draws more than sixty canine competitors and a thousand spectators from across the state and beyond. As with any sprint, the dogs line up at one end of the grass course and, on the starter's call, they are released by their owners and are supposed to race to the other end. 'It started off as a bit of fun,' says Port Fairy Winter Festival committee member John Watkinson, 'but now people take it quite seriously.' Unfortunately, the owners' determination to win is not always matched by that of their dogs. Some of the half-pint hounds are focused and will run straight to the other end, but others become distracted, wander off course to sniff spectators or each other, and have to be rescued by their embarrassed handlers. A few dig their paws in and refuse to budge an inch. 'There's not much training you can do,' admitted one owner. 'You just sit back and hope they'll run to the other end.'

The most dedicated owners elect to position friends or family members at the finish line armed with strips of bacon designed to lure their pets, but the strategy does not always work and, on average, around half the dogs fail to complete the course. The steeplechase event is more disciplined, simply because the owners guide the dogs around the course on leads. This sometimes involves physically lifting the dog over the low obstacle, which is as unedifying a spectacle as seeing A.P. McCoy climbing off his horse and lifting it over Becher's Brook.

FERRET LEGGING, YORKSHIRE, ENGLAND

Naturalists say that ferrets are never happier than when in dark, confined spaces, such as a rabbit hole or a drainpipe. Whether they are happy when thrust down the legs of a pair of trousers is open to question, but what is certain is that the gentleman wearing the trousers at the time is distinctly apprehensive. So it would seem bizarre – not to say masochistic – that anyone would voluntarily allow a predatory carnivore with razor-sharp teeth and claws like hypodermic needles to be inserted down their trousers. Yet that is what ferret legging is all about.

The quaint sport of ferret legging is an endurance test where two live ferrets are placed down a man's trousers, the goal being to survive for as long as possible and to emerge from the ordeal with one's dignity and manhood intact. Some sources suggest that the sport may have originated from poachers who used to keep their illicit hunting ferrets down their trousers to avoid detection by gamekeepers. It enjoyed something of a renaissance among Yorkshire coal miners in the 1970s, when public house patrons would bet on who could keep a ferret down his trousers the longest. Entertainment was clearly in short supply in 1970s Yorkshire. It also spread to Scottish culture, and the Richmond Highland Games and Celtic Festival in Virginia held an annual ferret-legging competition from 2003 to 2009. However, as recession and ferrets began to bite, contests became few and far between, and there are fears that the sport may soon vanish altogether.

The rules of ferret legging stipulate that trousers must be tied at the ankles and be loose enough to 'allow easy ferret access between the legs'. No underpants are permitted and male competitors 'whose families are not yet complete' must have written permission from their partner. The ferrets must have a full set of teeth and must not be sedated. Once the ferrets are inserted, the wearer's belt is pulled tight to prevent escape. Competitors can attempt, from outside their trousers, to dislodge the ferrets, but as the animals can maintain a strong hold for long periods their removal is no easy matter. Former world champion Reg Mellor used to wear white trousers so that he could show spectators the blood from the wounds caused by the ferrets. Reg was a showman. He was just what ferret legging needed.

A former Barnsley miner who attributed his success to ensuring that the ferrets were well fed before they were inserted into his trousers, Mellor set a new world record of five hours and twenty-six minutes at the annual Pennine Show in Holmfirth in 1981 at the age of seventy-one, by which time he had presumably concluded that his child-rearing days were behind him. Before he came along, the world record was a mere sixty seconds, which prompted Reg to exclaim: 'Sixty seconds! I can stick a ferret up me arse for longer than that!' Nobody, least of all a ferret, took him up on the offer. In 1986, he was well on his way to breaking the magical six-hour barrier until, after five hours, most of the 2,500 crowd became bored and started to drift away. Even though he protested that he was on his way to setting a new world record, workmen arrived to dismantle the stage. Disillusioned at such apathetic treatment of a national sporting icon, he retired on the spot. Lest you think that spending so many hours in close proximity to ferrets had given him an affection for the creatures, he once described them as 'cannibals, things that live only to kill, that'll eat your eyes out to get at your brain'. Hardly a glowing character reference.

Mellor's 1981 record stood until 2010 when sixty-seven-year-old retired headmaster Frank Bartlett and fellow villager Christine

Farnsworth managed to last for five hours thirty minutes at a ferret-legging contest in Whittington, Staffordshire. Inevitably there were mutterings about Ms Farnsworth's right to be named as a joint world record holder, as quite clearly she had less to lose in the contest. In the spirit of gender equality, an attempt had previously been made to introduce a female version of the sport, ferret busting, in which women placed ferrets down their blouses, but it proved unsuccessful.

JUMPING FROG JUBILEE, ANGELS CAMP, CALAVERAS COUNTY, CALIFORNIA, USA

Inspired by the Mark Twain story *The Celebrated Jumping Frog of Calaveras County*, since 1928 the community of Angels Camp has staged an annual Jumping Frog Jubilee in May. The contest to find the amphibian with the biggest leap quickly proved such a hit that it was incorporated into the Calaveras County Fair in the 1930s.

Those who take the contest seriously usually prefer to head out in the dead of night to catch their own frogs, while amateurs who are competing just for fun are happy to use rental frogs. The California bullfrogs for hire in the competition are caught locally in late spring and are fed on crickets to build up their strength. It is illegal to use specimens of the California red-legged frog in the competition as this is an endangered species. After the contest, the rental frogs are released back into the same pond where they were caught in the hope that they will grow into even more accomplished jumpers over the ensuing twelve months. To make sure that the bullfrogs do not get stressed or use up too much energy prior to the contest, calming music is played in their specially built 'frog spa' during the four days of the fair. Who knew that frogs were into easy listening? Frog welfare is always to the fore, with restrictions placed on the number of jumps each animal is asked to make per day.

First-time visitors to the fair may be alarmed to hear that the frogs have jockeys, but don't worry, nobody climbs on their backs. It is just a term for the entrant, who crouches behind the frog to encourage it to jump. Many of the more experienced jockeys work in family groups that have passed down frog-jumping secrets through generations of competition. These jockeys employ a range of techniques to coerce their frog into action, most of them designed to make the creature believe it is being hotly pursued by a hungry predator. Sheer terror rather than simply wanting to do well for one's jockey is clearly the force that motivates a frog to leap great distances. Some jockeys shout and jump or slap the ground while others prefer the more cerebral approach of blowing on their frog. In desperation, some will try all three.

The competition runs over all four days of the fair, with the top fifty jumpers progressing to the finals on the Sunday. All frogs must be at least four inches long from nose to tail and must start with all four feet, including toes, on the eight-inch launch pad. The distance is measured on the third jump in a straight line from the centre of the pad to the tail of the frog. A walk or skip is counted as a jump. During the jump, only the person jockeying the frog may move ahead of the launch pad, and any frog that does not jump within one minute of its start time will be disqualified. Whoever has the longest-jumping frog wins a $750 prize, or $5,000 if their frog manages to break the 1986 record of 21 foot 5¾ inches set by the amazing Rosie the Ribeter, the amphibian equivalent of Bob Beamon.

Rosie the Ribeter's jockey, Lee Giudici, a veteran of the contest, says that the frogs should be handled as little as possible beforehand because if they jump around too much, they will be too tired on the big day. They should not be kept too cool, either. When he first entered a frog at the Calaveras County Fair in his pre-Rosie days, Giudici admitted he did everything wrong. After finally catching a frog one night, he realised he did not know how to care for it, so he packed it on ice. However, since frogs are cold-blooded creatures, this had the effect of putting the animal into a state of semi-hibernation, which is not exactly ideal for jumping. 'We put the frog down on the pad, and it was asleep,' he lamented. He didn't make the same mistake again.

OSTRICH RACING, CHANDLER, ARIZONA, USA

With a top speed of over 40mph, long legs that can cover up to sixteen feet in a single stride, and a temperament that could best be described as irascible, an ostrich is not the easiest creature to ride. Bernie Clifton may have made it look reasonably straight-forward, but in reality the job of ostrich jockey ranks only slightly above crocodile dentist or skunk handler. Yet ostrich racing dates back to the days of ancient Egypt and still takes place in South Africa and at various American fairs, including the annual Chandler Ostrich Festival in Arizona.

First held in 1989, the March festival features two types of ostrich racing – bareback and with chariots. Both are started from stalls. In the former, helmeted riders, all of whom must weigh less than 150 pounds, sit precariously on the birds' spherical backs, and when the stalls open, they cling on for all their worth. There are no saddles, stirrups or reins, just a clump of wing bones to grip – like the handlebars on a bike. The jockey is immediately fighting battles on two fronts: trying to stay on the bird and attempting to persuade it to run towards the finish line rather than in any direction it fancies. With its high-stepping gait reminiscent of a Parisian can-can dancer, even the mildest ostrich is physically unbalanced when it runs, but an angry bird, with an uninvited passenger on its back, is mentally unbalanced, too. Consequently, many riders come to grief within a few strides of leaving the gate, deposited on the dirt track after being catapulted over the neck, sliding off the sides or falling off the back. There are almost as many ways to exit an ostrich as there are to leave your lover.

In theory, the chariot races should be less chaotic since the driver stands in a small cart that is towed along by the ostrich.

The driver steers by holding a broom next to the ostrich's head, causing the bird to turn away from the broom. So to make the ostrich turn left, the broom should be held to its right. However, the birds tend to overcompensate and as they veer wildly across the course, the connection between ostrich and chariot becomes tenuous at best, resulting in multiple pile-ups. Having unseated their riders, the ostriches prance menacingly around the arena until they are caught. Spectators near the fence are warned to watch out for kicks or sharp beaks. The birds are often blind-folded between races to keep them calm, but it doesn't seem to work too well. An ostrich without a strop is like a bear without a fur coat.

Speaking to ESPN, bird-racing veteran Dustin Murley offered this advice to prospective ostrich jockeys: 'Keep a leg on each side and your brain in the middle And if you fall, hope to God the bird don't fall with you.'

It would be all too easy to dismiss the ostrich as a crazy bird with a brain the size of a pea, which, having been gifted with strength and speed, had the good sense early in its existence to let humans know that it didn't much care for being a beast of burden. It was only too happy to let horses, camels and oxen do the donkey work. On the contrary, the ostrich may be a deceptively intelligent creature; it is the people who choose to ride them that are crazy.

PIG DIVING, CHANGSHA, HUNAN PROVINCE, CHINA

Pigs may not be able to fly as such, but they do a pretty good impression of it when they plunge from a high board into Shiyan Lake in Changsha, China, as part of a new May Day pig diving competition. After sailing gracefully through the air and landing safely in the water, the piglets, all with numbers painted on their backs, race each other to the shore, making this a test not only of diving ability but also of swimming speed. This is pork at its most versatile.

The contest organiser, Shi Huang, insists that the piglets are trained to dive, but the fact that their 'coaches' have to push them off the thirty-foot-high platform using boards suggests that it is not an activity that comes naturally. The ensuing swim to shore along a lane marked off on the lake with bamboo canes is tackled with greater relish, to the delight of the cheering spectators, and at the finish the competitors are handsomely rewarded with food – pearls of barley before swine.

Pig diving has been championed by a number of Chinese farmers, who claim that it makes the animals healthier, leaner . . . and tastier. Some have built special sloping platforms so that their pigs can enjoy a daily dive, and maintain that, although one or two may be a little hesitant to take the plunge, they lose their inhibitions once they see the rest go in. However, if you're expecting to see a hammy Tom Daley with artistic dives of varying degrees of difficulty, it should be remembered that pigs only seem to have mastered one dive, the belly pork flop.

Australia's Royal Melbourne Show has also staged demonstrations of pig diving and pig racing, and during the 2000s the **Pig Olympics** were staged in Shanghai (2005) and Moscow (2006). Events included pig racing over an obstacle course, pig swimming, and swineball, in which teams of five pigs played football by pushing the ball with their snouts and occasionally kicking it with their trotters. To encourage the animals to pursue the ball, it was covered in fish oil. A dozen piglets from seven countries took part in the 2006 Games and were spared the dinner table afterwards. Alexei Sharshkov, vice-president of the country's Sport-Pig Federation (motto 'From Rasher With Love'), told BBC News: 'They go on to produce a new generation of sport pigs. They don't get eaten. How could you eat a competitor who is known around the world?'

RABBIT SHOW JUMPING, SWEDEN

Until fairly recently, the rabbit's role in sport was very much on the receiving end – often of a twelve-bore shotgun wielded by individuals who stubbornly adhere to the belief that hunting defenceless animals somehow constitutes a leisure activity. Happily, some European countries have found a new outlet for rabbits in sport, and it is one that does not involve casseroles. Since it was first staged in Sweden in the late 1970s, rabbit show jumping – or *kaninhop* – has become one of the fastest-growing sports in Scandinavia. When it was introduced, the rules were based on those of horse show jumping, but they have subsequently been tailored so that they better meet the needs of rabbits. Thankfully, one of these was to make the fences considerably lower than for horses.

There are four different types of competitive rabbit jumping in Sweden – crooked course, straight course, high jump and long jump. The first two are similar to show jumping, with handlers guiding the domestic rabbits around the miniature obstacles on leads, the fastest clear round being the winner. The Swedish Federation of Rabbit Jumping stresses the need for happy bunnies: 'It is important that the rabbit jumps out of free will and isn't forced. The rabbit has to be in front of the owner. And remember, only the rabbit is to jump, the human walks beside the jumps and not over them.' Faults are incurred for knocking down a fence, jumping askew, and for lifting a rabbit over a fence that hasn't already been knocked down. Obstacles are graded in five levels – mini, easy, medium, difficult and elite – ranging in height from eight to thirty-one inches, according to the size and experience of the rabbit. The high jump and long jump are self-explanatory. The world rabbit high jump record is 39.37 inches by a

Swedish rabbit called Aysel. The world long jump record of 9.84 foot was set by a Danish rabbit, Yaboo. And that was without Elmer Fudd in hot pursuit.

The first Swedish national championships took place in Stockholm in 1987, and today competitions take place regularly across Europe, the United States and Australia. Breeders begin training their rabbits to jump by walking them on a harness from as early as eight weeks. They are advised to offer constant words of encouragement to the animals during both training and events, because, as one might expect with rabbits, the carrot works better than the stick.

The Finns dispense with animals altogether for their annual **National Hobbyhorsing Championship**, which takes place in Helsinki. The sport of hobbyhorsing is the same as conventional show jumping except that the rider jumps fences while straddling a stuffed toy horse on a wooden stick, complete with glued-on eyes and mane. Despite these adornments, it is impossible to get away from the fact that the competitors are essentially horsing around a ring on mops. For those ill equipped to tackle the three-foot-high obstacles, there is the more leisurely dressage competition, where the judges award marks for artistry, elegance and nimble footwork. Naturally, dressage participants insist on looking the part and many wear their finest equestrian regalia of top hat and tails. Hard though it may be to believe, there are as many as ten thousand active hobbyhorsers in Finland, ranging from young children to grown-ups who should know better. It appears to be the ideal sport for people who have always wanted to ride but who find horses just a wee bit scary . . . and who don't mind being considered, shall we say, different.

SHEEP COUNTING, BREDASDORP, SOUTH AFRICA

Sheep farming is such an integral part of rural life in many countries that, following national contests to find the fastest shearer, it was only a matter of time before someone devised a sheep-counting competition. The format sees a vast flock of up to four hundred sheep rush across a field past a line of humans, and whoever counts them the most accurately – without falling asleep – is declared the winner. It's a bit like a mobile, woolly version of the 'guess the weight of the cake' contests that are so popular at village fetes.

The idea stemmed from auction-yard workers who routinely have to count over a hundred thousand sheep every day, and the first official sheep-counting competition was held in Dewetsdorp, South Africa in 1984. It went on to become a fixture at many South African shows, one of the biggest being the annual contest at Bredasdorp as part of Agri Mega Week in September.

With so many sheep to choose from, naturally the concept soon took off in Australia and in 2002, hundreds of spectators flocked to the first Australian National Sheep Counting Championships at Hay, New South Wales. Peter Desailly beat off 100 rivals by correctly counting 277 sheep. Experienced Australian sheep counter Mark Jacka said: 'It sounds pretty simple, like anyone could do it, but it's pretty tough. In my work, I count up to 60,000 sheep a day as they enter and exit auction yards. You end up counting 120,000 sheep. You sleep pretty well after that.'

Sheep-racing events take place at various locations across the UK, including The Big Sheep attraction near Bideford, Devon, which features daily sheep races in summer. Six sheep with names such as Red Ram, Sheargar and Woolly Jumper, sprint along a 250-yard course. Since 2012, the **Moffat Sheep Races** have been run every year along the Dumfries and Galloway town's High Street in August to celebrate the local wool industry. Each sheep carries a small knitted jockey – a Woolly Carson – on its back and attempts to clear a series of low obstacles without unseating its rider. There is often a certain amount of reluctance at the start – at least until the appearance of a sheepdog begins to focus minds. Even then, progress can be painfully slow as sheep do what they do best and blindly follow each other, whether it be to the next fence or into the local Gregg's. If the sheep continue circling aimlessly for so long that even the sheepdog has lost interest, human handlers are introduced to gee them along. Spectators are able to bet on the outcome of the six heats and the final, having no doubt closely studied the sheep form book to make sure they don't get fleeced.

WORLD DOG SURFING CHAMPIONSHIPS, PACIFICA, CALIFORNIA, USA

From the moment Man first discovered the joys of surfing the waves, it was inevitable that sooner or later he would ask his best friend to join him – even if that best friend has four legs, a wet nose and a strange attraction to lampposts. Now every summer in a series of competitions around California, dogs of all breeds, shapes and sizes jump on surfboards and take to the sea in the hope of catching some waves and impressing the human judges. There are categories for dogs who solo surfboard, dogs who ride the board in tandem with another dog, and dogs who share the board with their owner. Whatever the format, their aim is to stay on the board for as long as possible, ride as many waves as they can, and, perhaps most important of all for any surfer, look cool.

Surfing dogs have been reported around California, Hawaii and Florida since the 1920s. Dave Chalmers and his surfing terrier Max, from San Diego, became media darlings in the 1980s, making film and TV appearances. As more and more dogs started taking to the water, in 2006 the Loews Coronado Bay Resort in Imperial Beach, California staged its first dog-surfing competition. Animals, some wearing Hawaiian shirts, wetsuits and sunglasses, competed in ten-minute heats and were judged on confidence level, length of ride, fashion, and their ability to 'grip it and rip it'. Judge Kathleen Cochran told Reuters: 'I personally look for attire, whether they come dressed seriously with board shorts on, what's going on with their tails, whether they're wagging them. For me, that means they're having fun and that's what this is all about.'

A prolific champion in the small dog category has been Abbie, an Australian kelpie owned by Michael Uy, who credits surfing with turning Abbie from a traumatised rescue dog into a loving pet. He used to take her to the beach near San Diego to build up her confidence among other dogs, and she soon started following him into the water and jumping on his board. One day, he allowed her to float with the wave and when she didn't fall off, her competitive surfing career was born. She wears a wetsuit made of the same material used by US Navy Seals, and her exceptional balance and determination has enabled her to ride six-foot-high waves. She rides a custom-designed fibreglass board and her nails are kept longer before a competition so that she can obtain a better grip on the board. Instead of just standing motionless, she has even mastered moves used by professional surfers. 'She's figured out how to trim the board,' says her proud owner, 'moving around to get the balance right to stay on the wave or steer, and can also sometimes cut across the face of a big wave.' To keep in shape, Abbie and Uy surf for up to two hours a day and go on seven-mile runs together. In 2011, she went into *Guinness World Records* for the longest wave surfed by a dog when she surfed a 351-foot wave at Ocean Beach, and three years later she became the first dog to be inducted into the International Surfing Hall of Fame.

With more than sixty dogs regularly demonstrating their skills at the Loews event, it had been regarded for years as the premier dog-surfing competition. However, in September 2016 the first World Dog Surfing Championships were staged further up the coast near San Francisco and it is now a bone of contention as to which is the more prestigious. Naturally Abbie became the first official world champion, pushing Brandy the pug into second place. All those hours of dedicated training and abstaining from chasing cats up trees had paid off.

WORLD SNAIL RACING CHAMPIONSHIPS, CONGHAM, NORFOLK, ENGLAND

The World Snail Racing Championships have the distinction of being the most leisurely race you are ever likely to witness. It is Formula 1 with the handbrake on. At a shout of 'Ready, Steady, Slow', the supercharged molluscs slug it out every July to find which of them is the fastest to complete the marathon thirteen-inch course. The winning time is usually around three and a half minutes, an average speed of 0.0032mph. For the snails, the whole race passes by in a flash.

The event was founded in the 1960s by farmer Tom Elwes, who had observed snail racing at close quarters in France, where they love to put the 'go' into *escargot*. He brought the idea back to the Norfolk village of Congham, a hotbed of snail reproduction, to raise money for the local church. Championship official Hilary Scase told the *Daily Telegraph*: 'Snails like damp conditions and as Congham is surrounded by ponds and is very low lying, it is just right for snails. Congham is to snail racing what Newmarket is to horse racing.'

Entrants can either bring their own snail or choose one from the local talent pool. More than two hundred snails – with identifying numbers stuck to their shells – take part in a series of heats followed by the grand final. The races take place on a table that is covered with a damp cloth. This is kept well watered throughout the day to stimulate high speeds. For each race, fifteen snails are placed in the centre of an inner circle, from which they must travel thirteen inches to the outer circle that forms the finish line. Unfortunately, some of the snails – perhaps unaware that they are in a race – show more interest in each other than in reaching the finish. A loved-up snail is not a good racer; it is like Usain Bolt stopping halfway through the 100 metres because a pretty girl in the crowd has caught his eye. Once the snails are on their marks at the start, their owners must not touch them, although verbal encouragement is recommended. A shy snail will never be a champion. You have to bring them out of their shells, not least because it is the only way they can move.

Once owners find a champion snail, they often release it after the event into their garden in the hope that they can race either it or one of its many offspring the following year. Everyone is looking for a snail with a good racing pedigree. Snailmaster Neil Riseborough, who acts as the official starter for each race, breeds thousands of snails each year and trains them for the world championships by giving them an exhausting workout on tall French windows, followed by a meal of lollo rosso lettuce. The winning owner receives a silver tankard filled with lettuce.

The time they all want to beat is the far-from-sluggish two minutes twenty seconds set by a snail named Archie in 1995. The 2008 championships were won by Heikki Kovalainen, a snail named after the Finnish Formula 1 driver, but tragedy marred the 2016 event when the reigning champion, George, died suddenly – and some say mysteriously – the day before he was due to defend his title.

Nevertheless Riseborough is proud of the event's credentials. 'It's a good clean sport,' he told the *Telegraph*, 'and fortunately we've not had any doping scandals yet. No snail has failed a random slime sample.'

Controversially, the French village of Lagardere has also staged a World Snail Racing Championship for over thirty years, but that is a ruthless event in which every competitor bar the winner ends up cooked with ham, garlic and tomatoes and served to the spectators. All a snail gets for finishing second is a sudden sizzling sensation and the smell of hot butter, a last bitter memory for falling short of victory. 'I would never do that,' says Riseborough. 'I love them and nurture them. Treat a snail like any other pet and it will perform for you.'

INDEX